A Moment in Time

Fine Art Photography & Poetry

Capturing Creation as it Happens

Author: Dianne E. Woods

DEDICATION

Dedications are so special because they speak from the heart a message of love to supporters of a work. I would like to dedicate this fine arts and photography book to all those who are writers, poets, and photographers. Keep writing and taking pictures that captures moments in time that can never be duplicated, and share your gifts and talents with the world. This work is also dedicated to the many missions projects I support as a portion of the proceeds from the sale of this work is donated towards supporting local, national, and international missions projects that touch the lives of people in need.

POETRY TITLES

ACKNOWLEDGMENTS

I would like to acknowledge and give a special thanks to those that have encouraged me along this path to sharing my love for the arts through photography and poetry. Thank you Debra K. Williams for the hours you have spent encouraging me, and your constant willingness to consult on the many decisions I had to make while proofing this work. It has truly been a "journey to success" getting this first work together and you along with my family and friends have been in my thoughts and heart as I continued to put this together. Thank you all. Much love and appreciation!

Introduction

Let me share a little story with you how and why this photography and poetry book came about. One day I was downloading photographs on to my computer, something I always do on a regular basis, and happened to see the photo count, 6,890 (and counting). I paused for a moment and then it dawned on me, "you have over six thousand pictures on this computer and no one is enjoying them but you." These photos were taking during mission trips to Honduras, Haiti, The Dominican Republic, Bulgaria, Peru, personal travel to Israel and Paris, as well as my neighborhood walks, visits to the local parks and a myriad of activities of which I participate on a regular basis.

Every second of my day is filled with an opportunity to capture images streaking by in a moment in time. With my emotions stirred I decided to share with you the beauty I see in the world. A fresh fire was ignited as I began to print my favorite photographs, but it did not stop there, it was still another hidden part of me that needed to be revived, writing poetry. Many years ago wrote poetry that reflected every aspect of my life, friend, family, politics, love, hate, everything. It truly was a chronicle of my life experiences.

During a distressing time in my life all of my poetry and many of my photographs were destroyed. When that work was ruined, I felt all the life was sucked out of me, that part of my intimate life that I could never get back. It was dead and buried! As I talked with a friend about how I used to write, it became clear to me I still loved poetry and that gift was still there. When writing the works that proceed the images I felt once again that I had something to share with the world. My heartfelt interpretation, and how I see and feel about what surrounds me was rekindled, hence the title "A Moment in Time Fine Art Photography and Poetry." The title expresses how I feel about capturing photographs, and vividly describes the images...a moment in time... a second, a flash, a fleeting nanosecond that only passes through the planet once. I am capturing creation as it happens and writing about it from the heart.

There is nothing in life we see, feel, taste, touch, hear, or imagine that can ever be identically repeated or reproduced. Realizing everything in life is not always pleasant, capturing a moment in time through a photographic image or poetry, can help us engage with the beauty, and things that are not so beautiful, that oftentimes eludes us because of all the negativity and sorrow in our world. My heart for you, as you meander through the pages of this book, is to connect you with the poetry and visual message of each poem and picture. To further expand your grasp on some of the key words within the poems, I defined them with Webster's 1828 Dictionary. Enjoy!

Broken But Not Destroyed
By: Dianne E. Woods

Cracked and crushed and ripped and torn,
Broken but not destroyed.

Beaten down with time and change,
Broken but not destroyed.

What a time it used to be, in my glory days,
But now look at me, see my plight,
Broken but not destroyed.

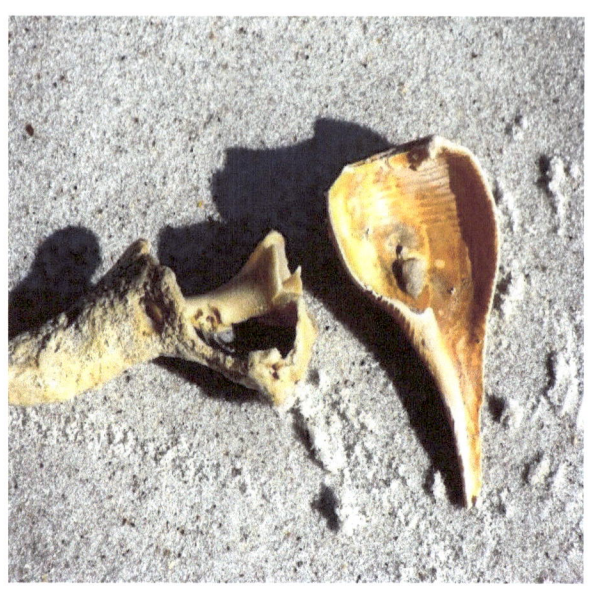

Fernandina Beach, Florida – November 2011

Still useful to some extent, my purpose rearranged,
In many ways my usefulness fades,
Broken but not destroyed.

Webster's 1828 Definitions:

Broken: *Parted by violence; rent asunder; infirm; made bankrupt.*

Destroyed: *Demolished; pulled down; ruined; annihilated; devoured; swept away; etc.*

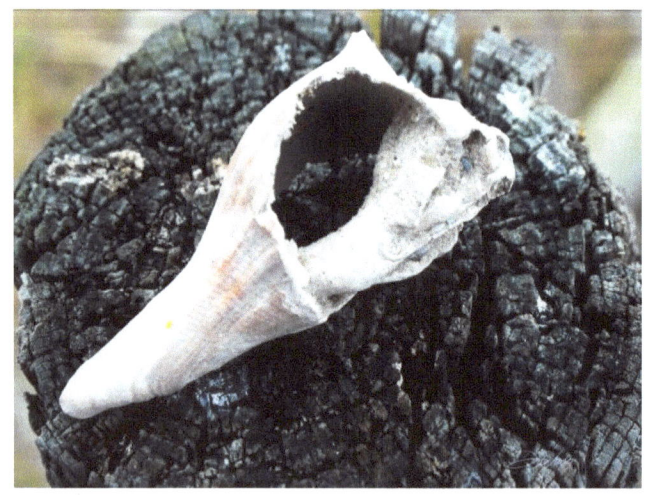

Huguenot Memorial Park, Jacksonville, FL December 2012

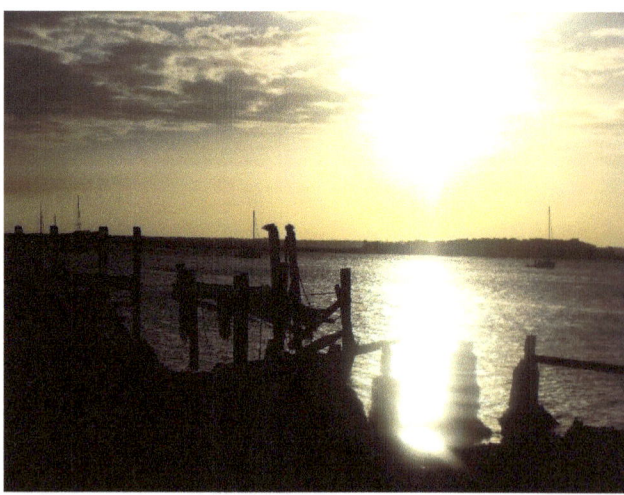

Fernandina Beach, Florida, November 2011

Poem: Broken But Not Destroyed

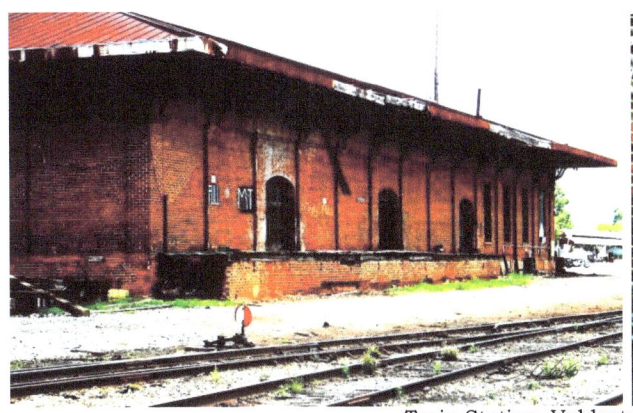 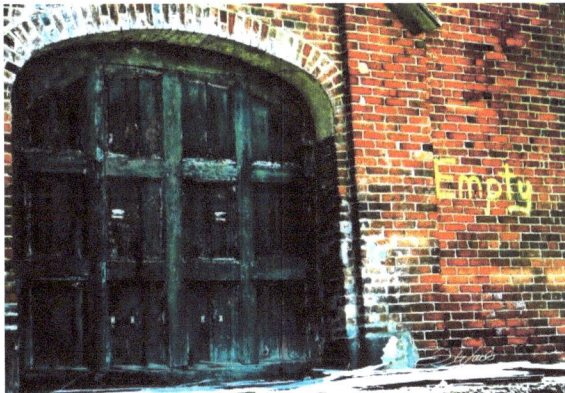

Train Station, Valdosta, Georgia, May, 2012

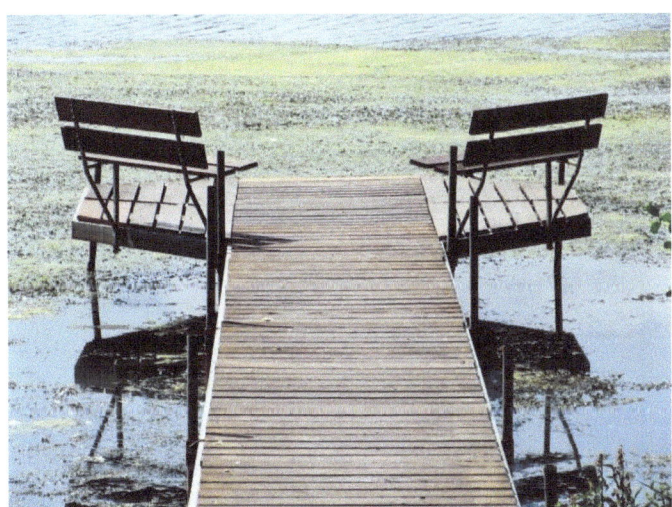

St. Paul, Minnisota, July 2014

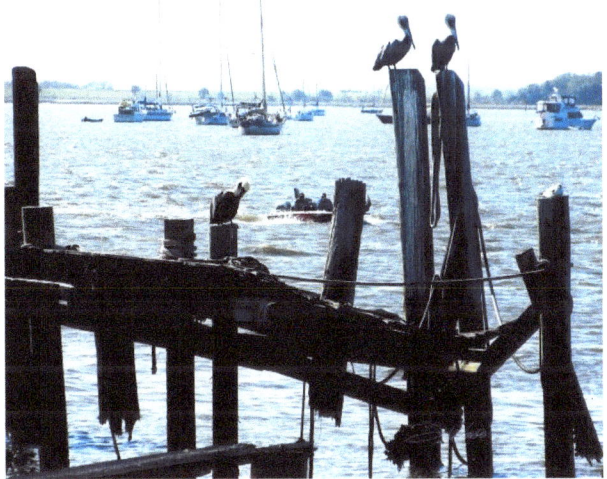

Fernadina Beach, Florida, November 2011

Poem: Broken But Not Destroyed

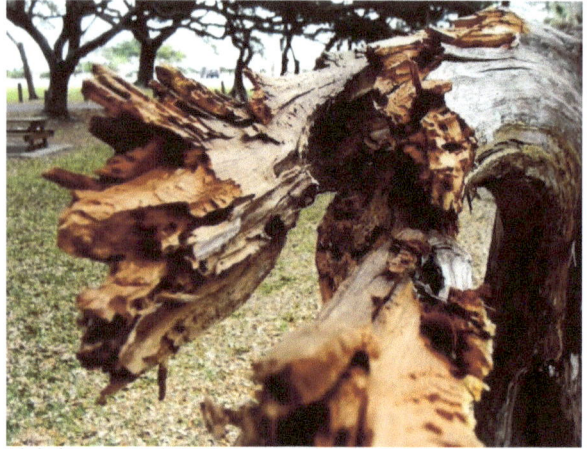

Lighthouse Park in St. Augustine Florida, December 2013

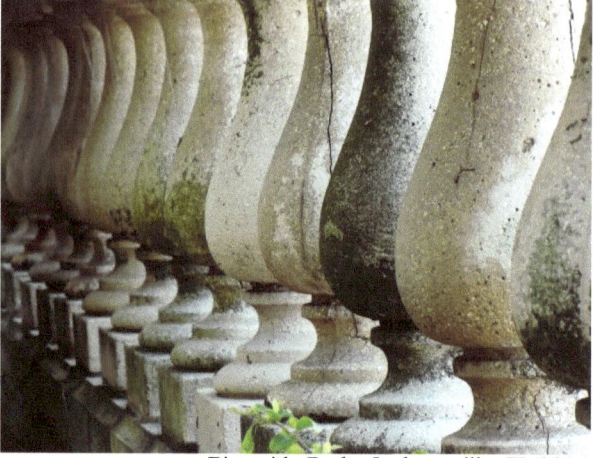

Riverside Park, Jacksonville, FL 2014

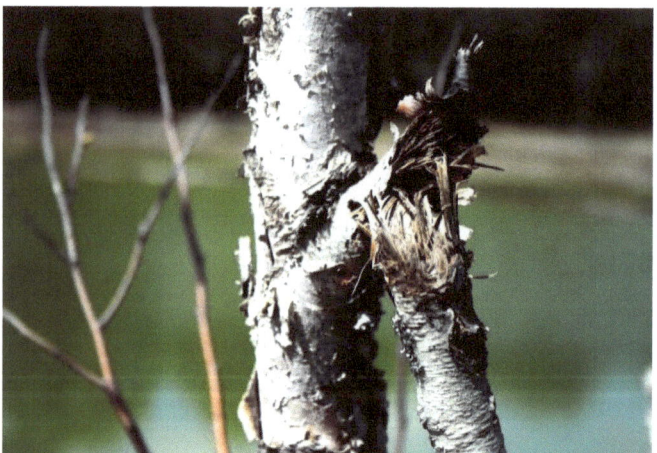

PAL Park, Jacksonville, Florida, March 2012

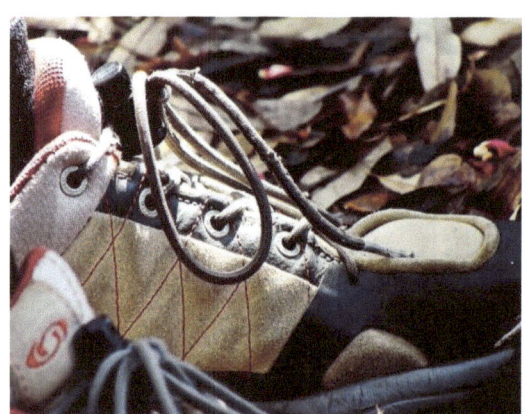

Riverside Park, Jacksonville, Florida, July, 2014

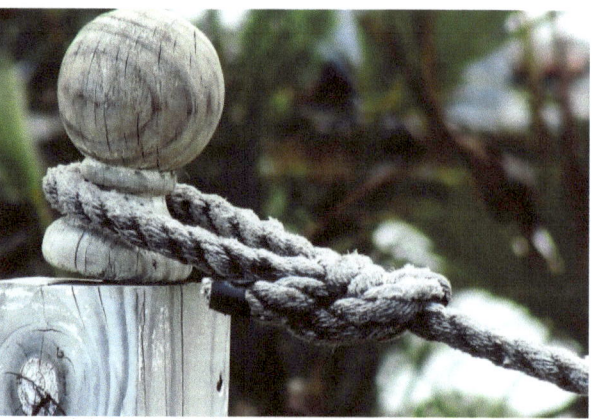

Lighthouse Park, St. Augustine Florida, July 2014

Telling The Story of Wind
By: Dianne E. Woods

Look at the skies, so majestic and high,
Telling the *story* of wind,
Clouds so big, clouds so bright,
Telling the *story* of wind.

Look at the skies, clouds rolling by,
Telling the *story* of wind,
Gentle and soft, breezy and still,
Telling the *story* of wind.

Rain or snow, angry winds that blow,
Telling the *story* of wind,
Day or night, dark or light,
Telling the *story* of wind.

Never a second the skies do not speak,
Telling the *story* of wind,
What do you see, as clouds go by?
Telling the *story* of wind.

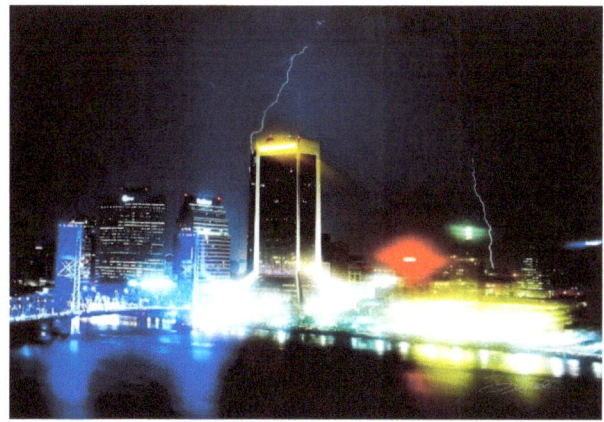

Jacksonville, Florida April 2012

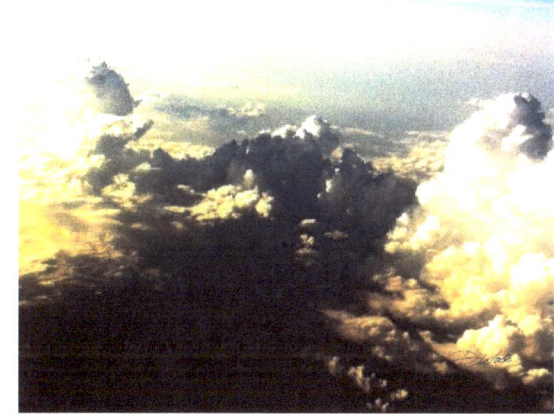

Flying High, July 2013

Webster's 1828 Definition:
Story: *A verbal narration or recital of a series of facts or incidents.*
Wind: A natural movement of air of any velocity; the earth's air surrounding the planet in natural motion horizontally.

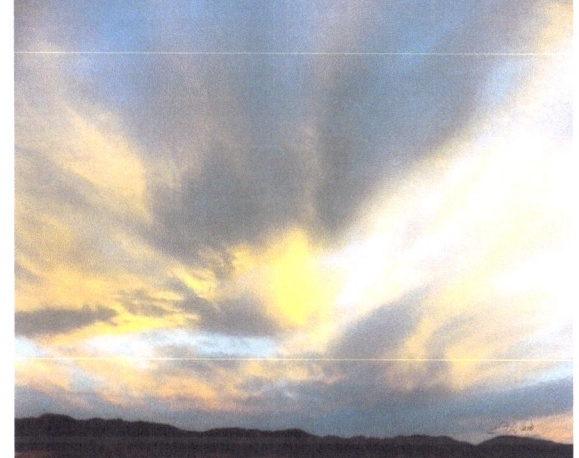

Colorado Rockies, July 2013

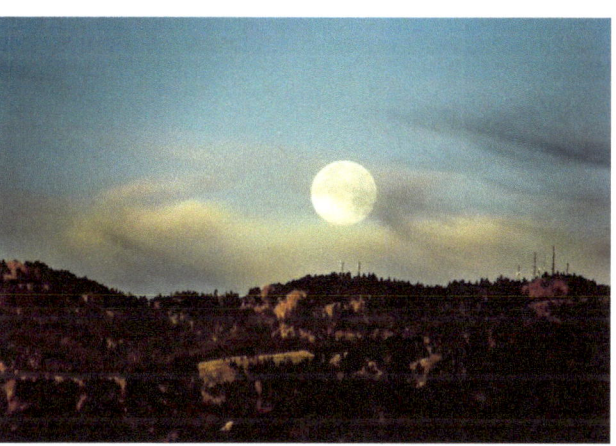

Colorado Rockies, July 2013

Poem: Telling the Story of Wind

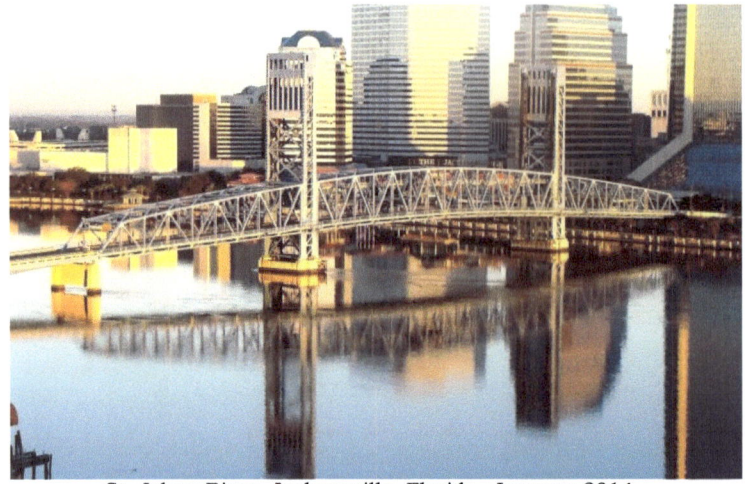

St. Johns River, Jacksonville, Florida, January 2014

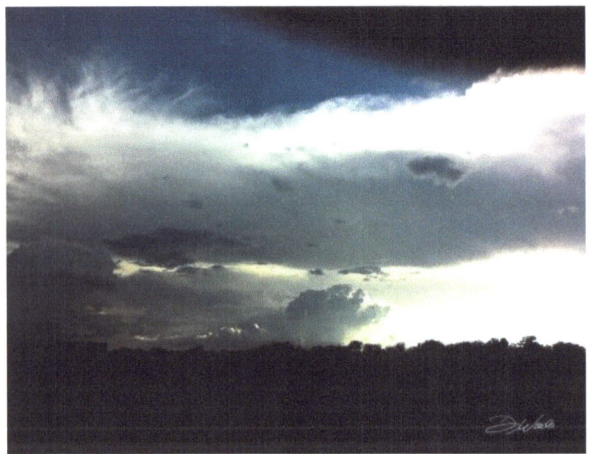

Macon, Georgia, July 2012

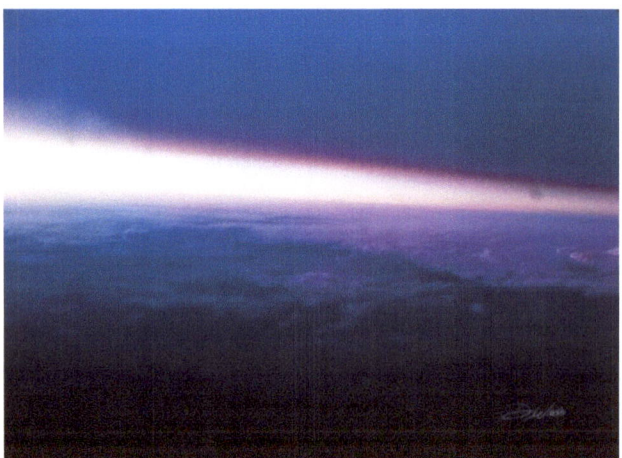

Evening Sky July 2013

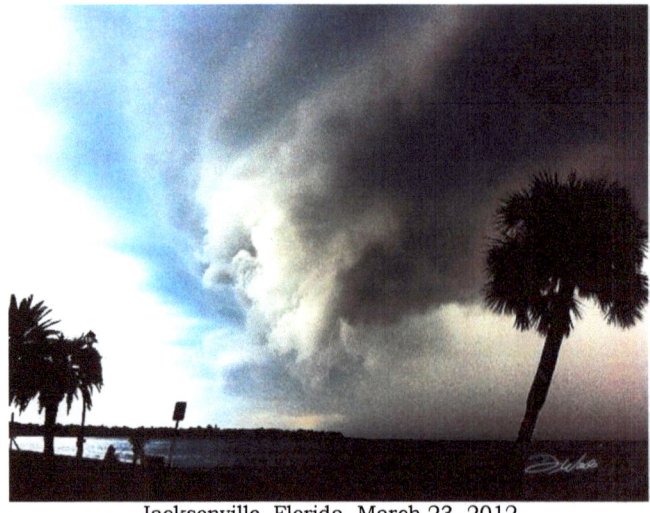

Jacksonville, Florida, March 23, 2012

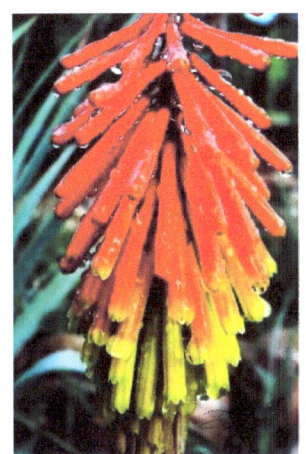
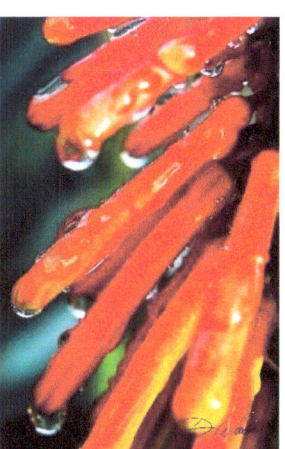

Dew Drops In
By: Dianne E. Woods

Only once will you pass my way,
Appearing, disappearing, daily falling away.

You come and you go, I know not where,
But I count on you, to always be there.

With your tiny touch, you gleam and glimmer,
Like a mini mirror, you reflect and shimmer.

Your time is brief, your touch so sweet,
But I always know, every day we'll meet.

Webster's 1828 Dictionary Definition:
Dew: *The water or moisture collected or deposited on or near the surface of the earth, during the night, by the escape of the heat which held the water in solution.*

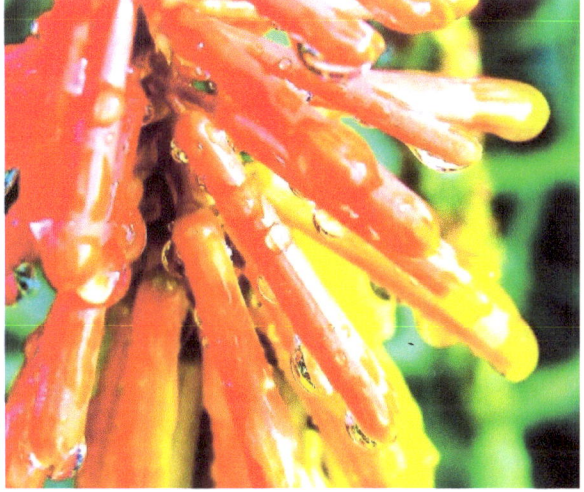

Colorado State University, July 2013

Poem: Dew Drops In

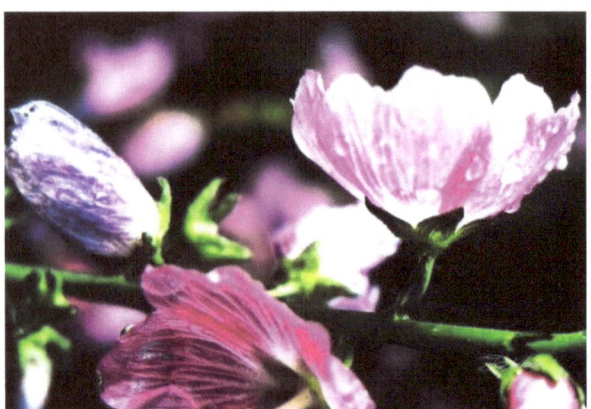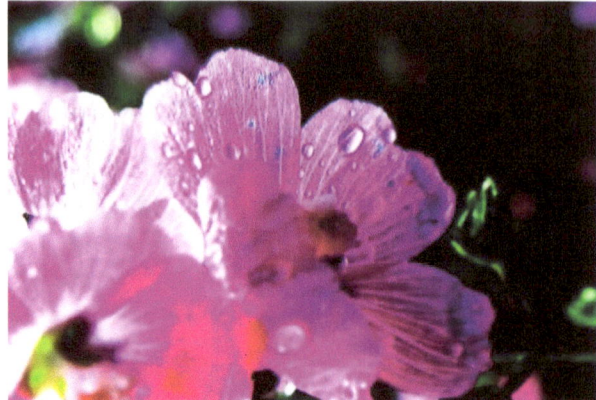

Photographed July, 2013

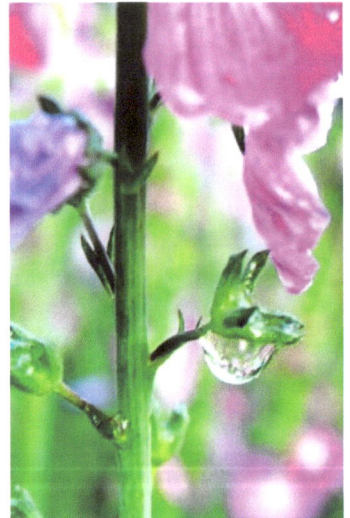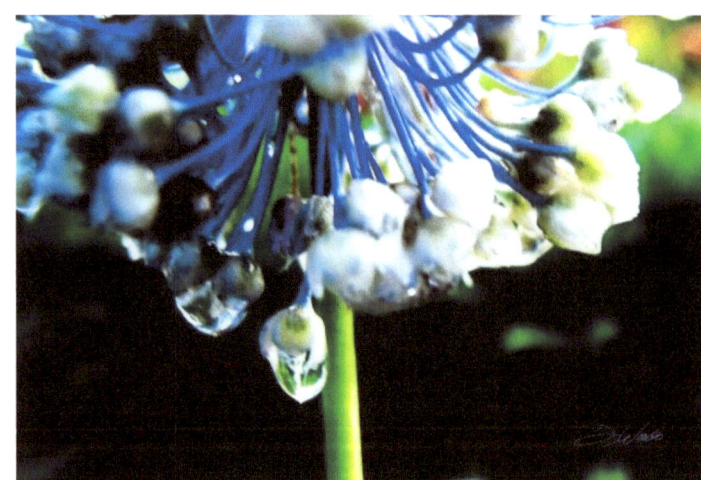

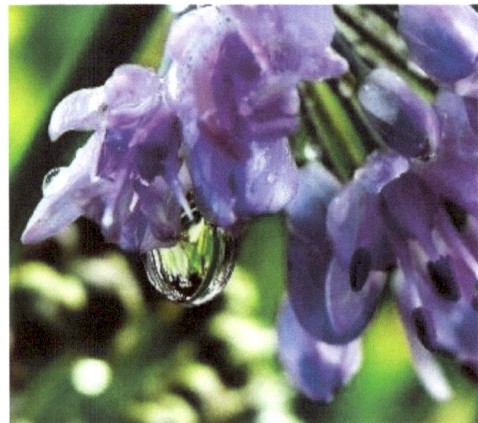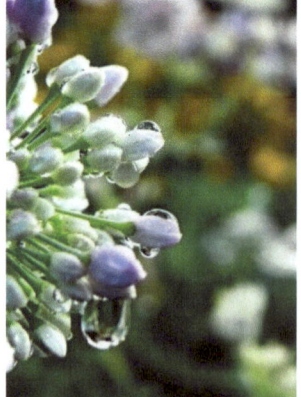

Colorado State University July 2013

Poem: Dew Drops In

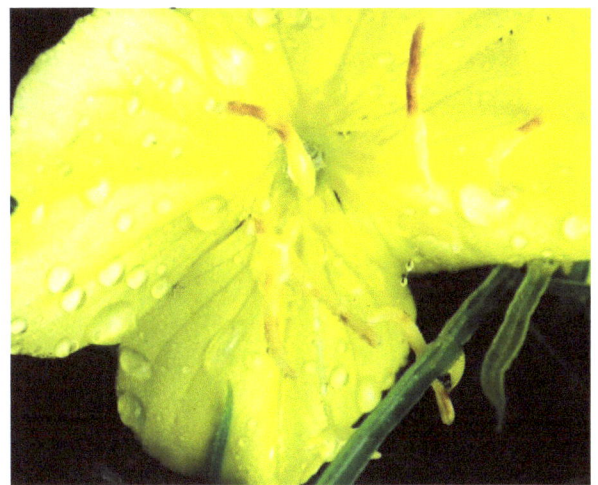

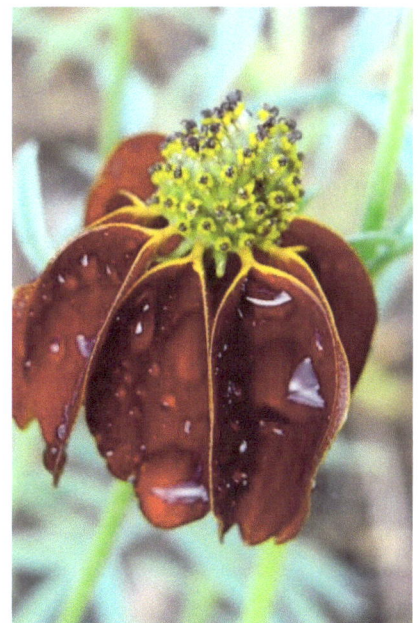

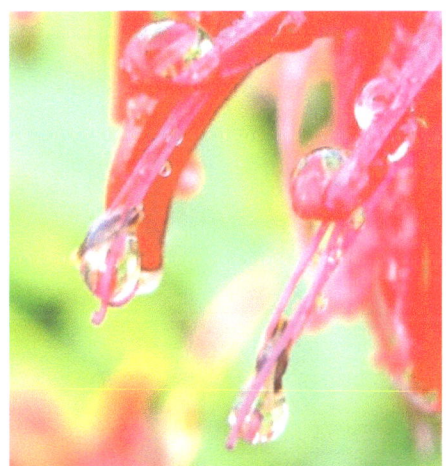

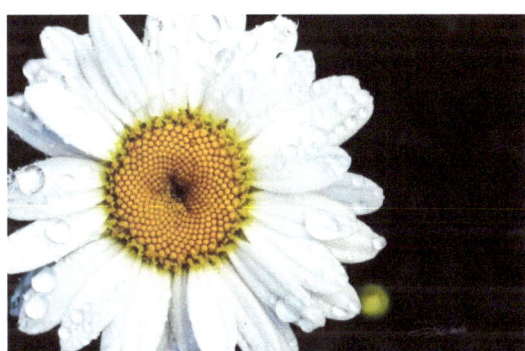

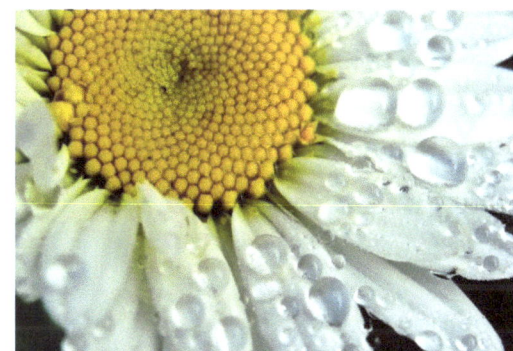

Colorado University, July 2013

9

Stuff from Everywhere

By: Dianne E. Woods

Stuff is not *really* stuff,
It's part of someone's life.
It comes from near, it comes from far,
It's part of someone's life.

How many times used or unused,
It's part of someone's life.
The things they loved and cherished,
It's part of someone's life.

Not valuable to me,
It's part of someone's life.
The memories you'll never see,
It's part of someone's life.

Call it junk, trash, treasure, or stuff,
It's part of someone's life.
And one day your stuff will be,
Part of someone's life.

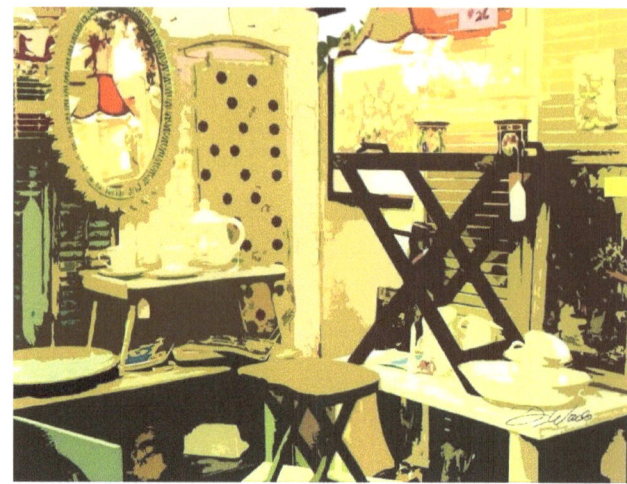

Antique Mall, Jacksonville, Florida, December 2013

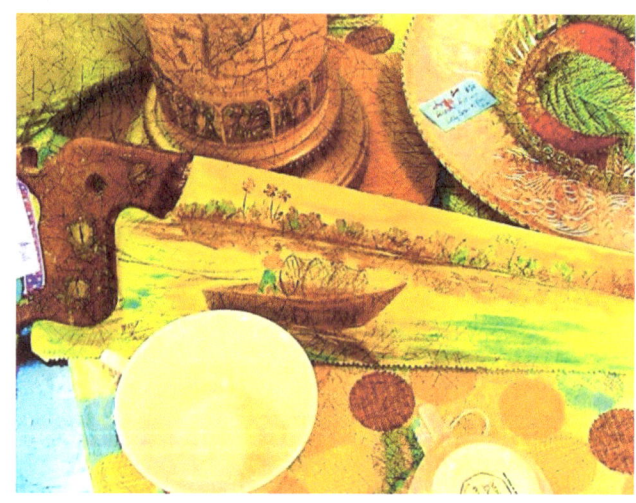

Webster's 1828 Dictionary Definition:
Stuff: *Furniture; goods; domestic vessels in general.*
Everywhere: *In every place; in all places.*

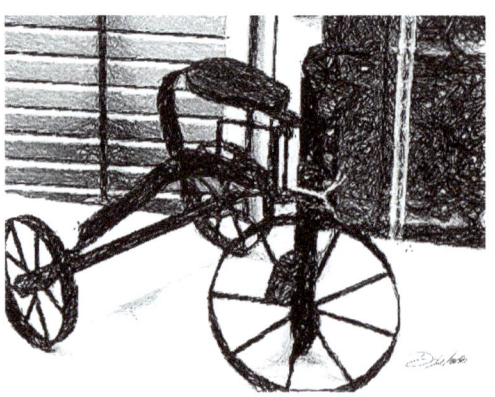

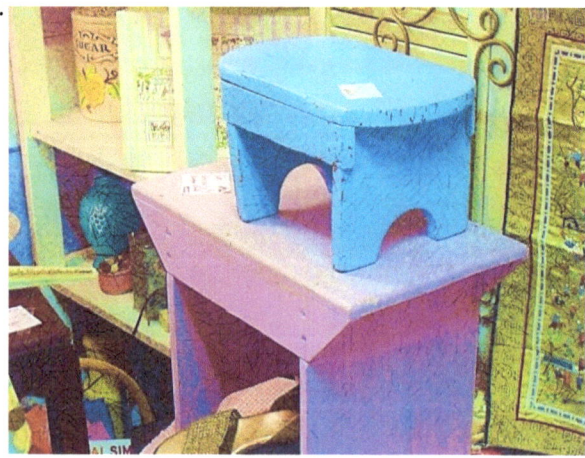

Antique Mall, Jacksonville, Florida, December 2013

Poem: Stuff from Everywhere

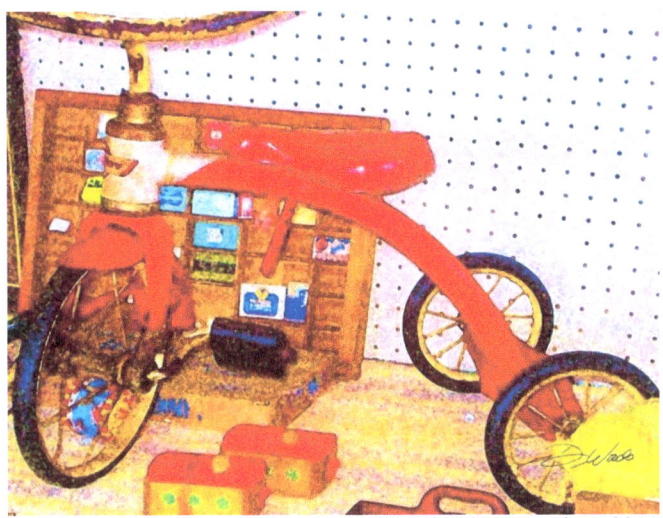

Bayard Antique Mall Jacksonville, Florida December, 2013

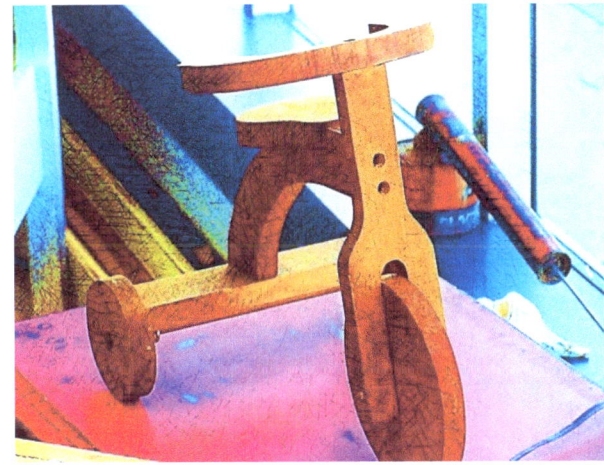

Antique Mall, Georgia, January 2013

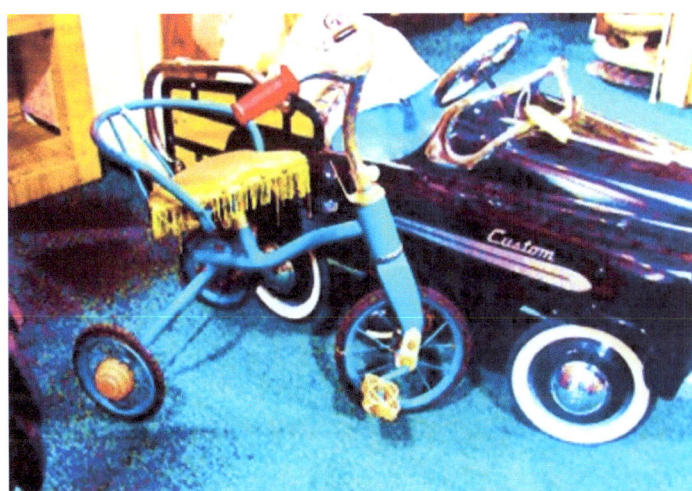

Antique Mall Julington Creek, Florida, February 2014

Poem: Stuff from Everywhere

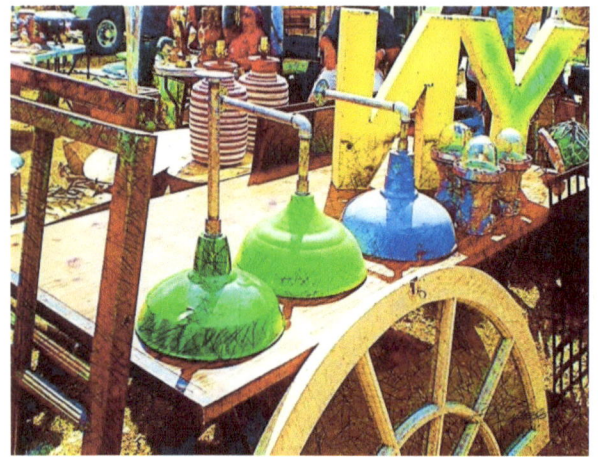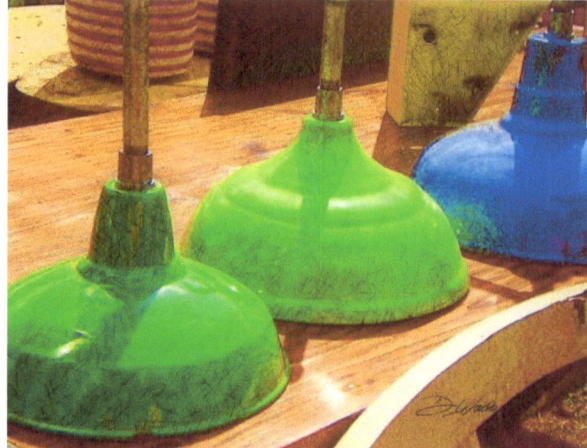

One of the largest flea market events in Florida February, 2012

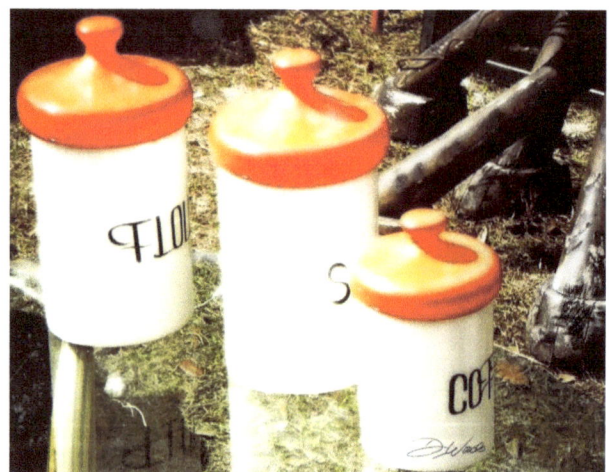

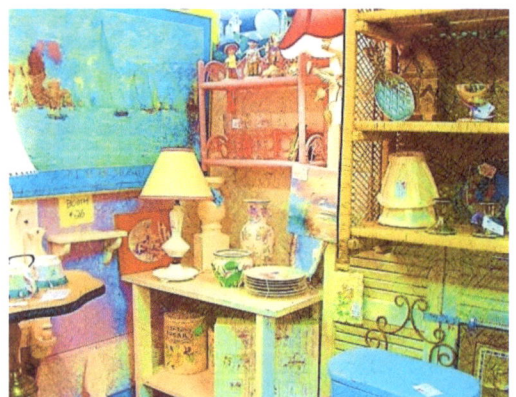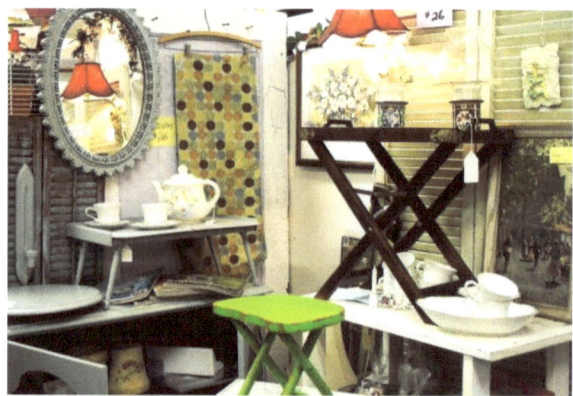

Antique Mall, Jacksonville, Florida, January 2012

Monocotyledons (The Orchid)

By: Dianne E. Woods

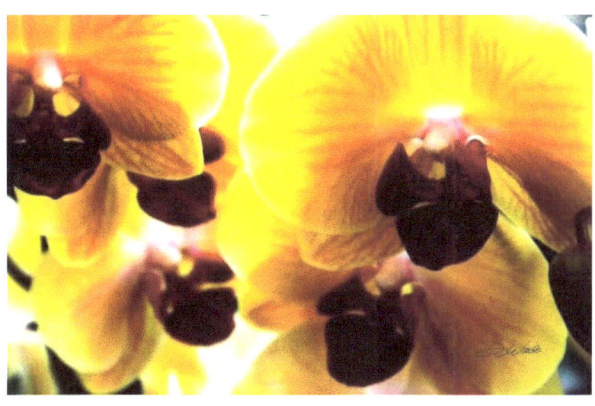

Details, Details, Details,
So many things to see,
When you look into my face
The orchid...that is me.

Stripes and dots and lines and curves,
My colours unsurpassed.
When you look into my face,
Move quick, cause it won't last.

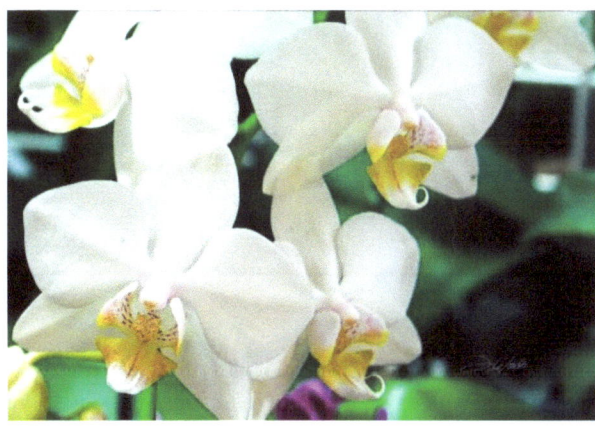

Take the time to study me,
What pictures can you find.
When you look into my face,
It's all within your mind.

Webster's 1828 Dictionary Definition:

Monocotyledons: *(another name for orchid) Having only one seed-lobe or seminal leaf. Orchid: plants that usually have showy 3 pedalled flowers with the middle petal enlarged into a lip and differing from the others in shape and colour*

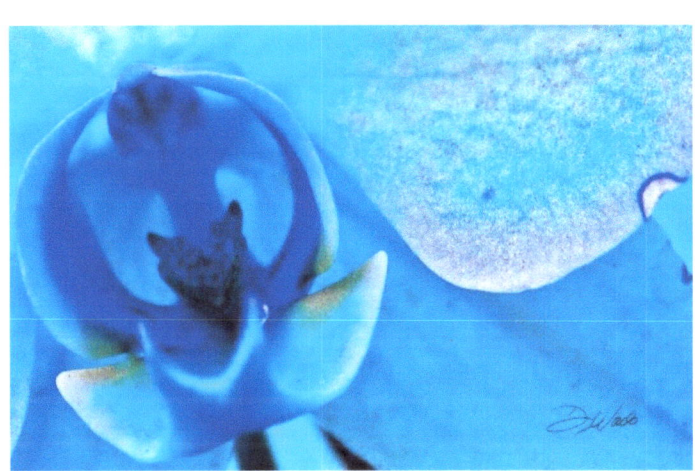

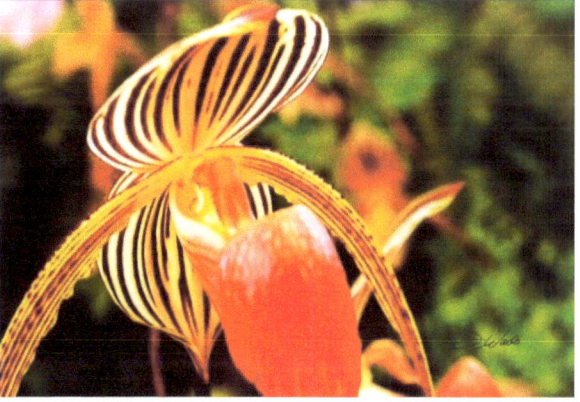

Orchid Show, Jacksonville, Florida, March, 2013

Poem: Monocotyledons (The Orchid)

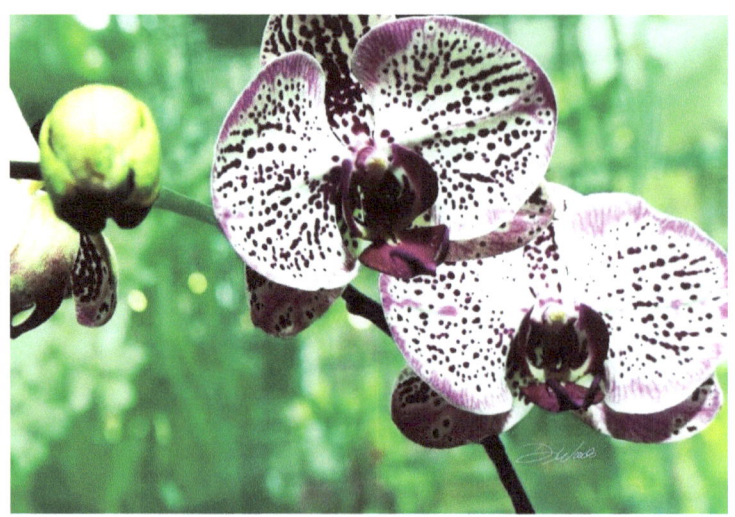

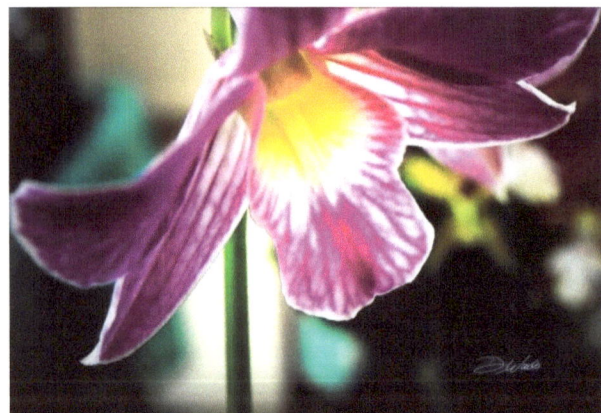
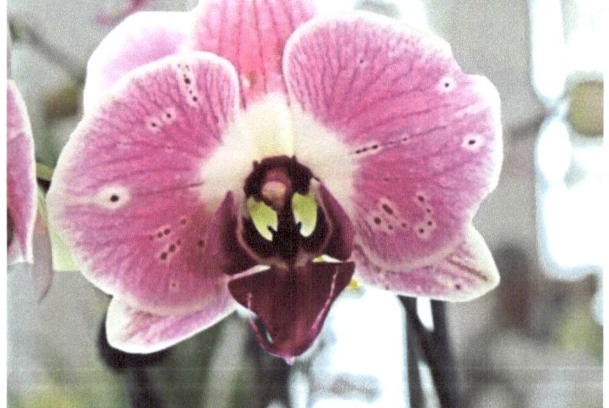

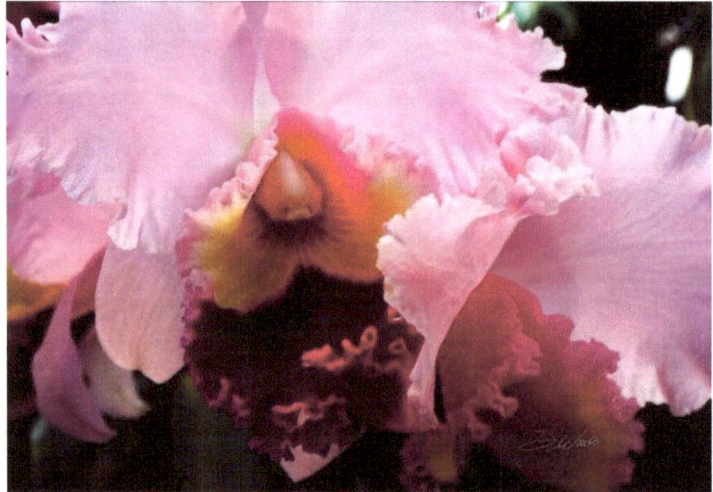

Orchid Show Jacksonville, Florida, March, 2013

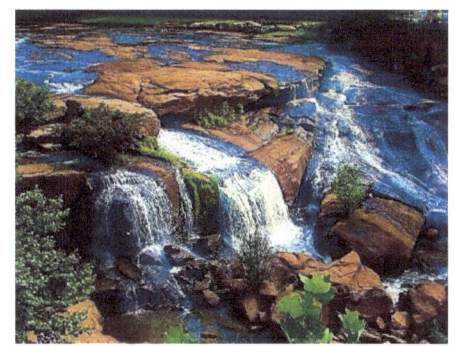

Water....Works
By: Dianne E. Woods

My assignment is unending, and I will tell you why,
Without me everything on earth, would be so very dry,
I'm constantly on the move, and always rushing by,
Morning, noon or night I'm there, but gone in the blink of an eye.

What are my assignments? Well think of it in this way,
When you looked into the sky, did it rained today?
I never tire of what I do, I touch the lives of many,
My gushing streams, my water falls, my lakes, have you seen any?

I carry life, you do not see, and that's my daily chore,
I stretch myself throughout the earth, my reach from shore to shore.
I cook, I clean, I wash, I play, each and every day,
My assignment is unending and will never go away.

Webster's 1828 Dictionary Definition:
Water: *A fluid, the most abundant and most necessary for living beings of any in nature, except air. water when pure, is colourless, destitute of taste and smell, ponderous, transparent, and in a very small degree compressible.*

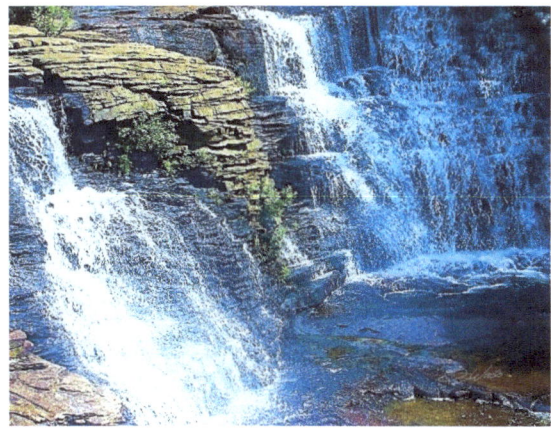

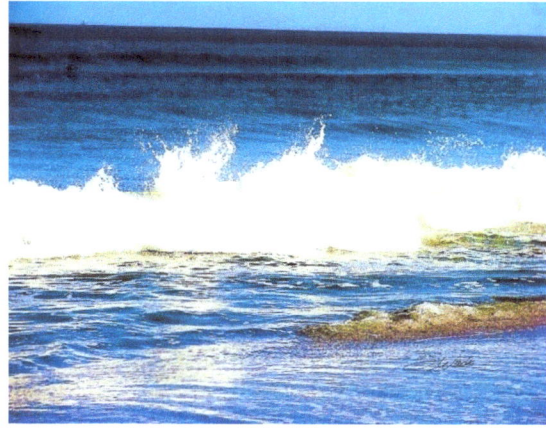

Poem: Water...Works

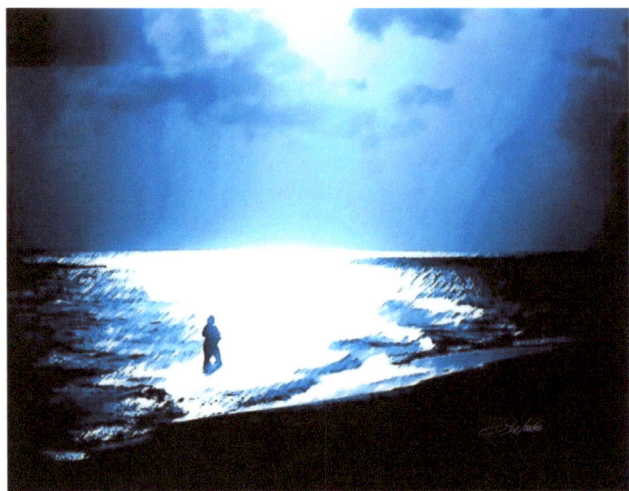

Les Cayes Haiti, August 2007

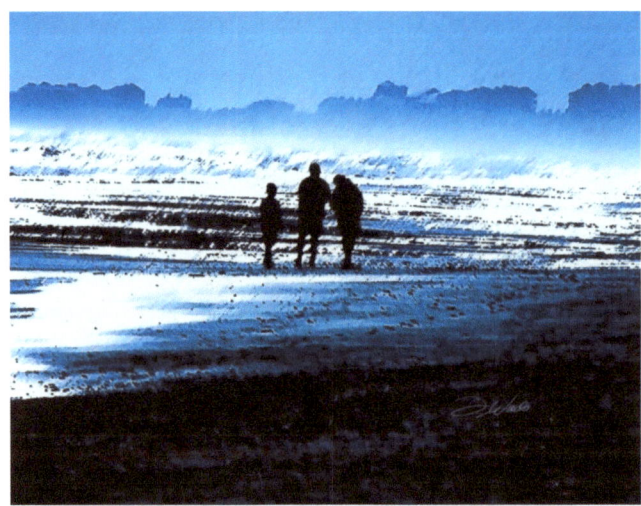

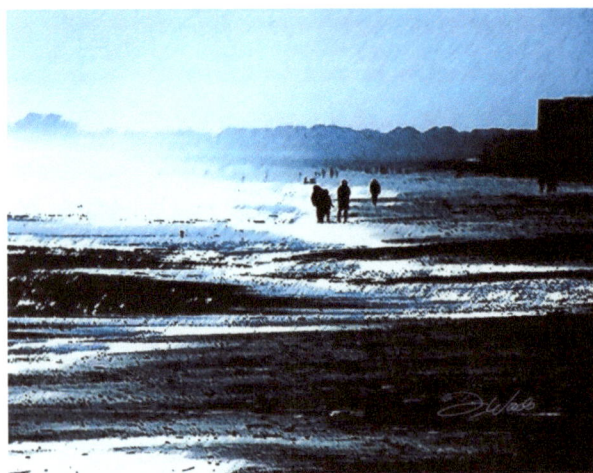 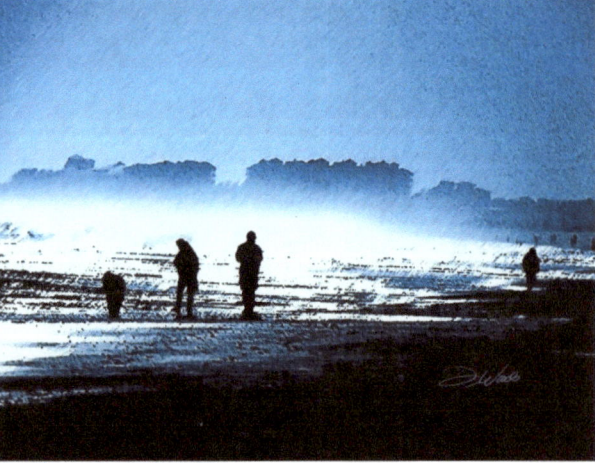

Fernandina Beach, Florida, November 25, 2011

Poem: Water...Works

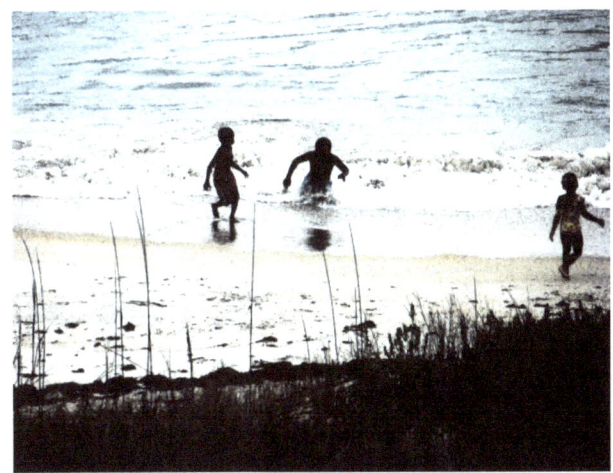 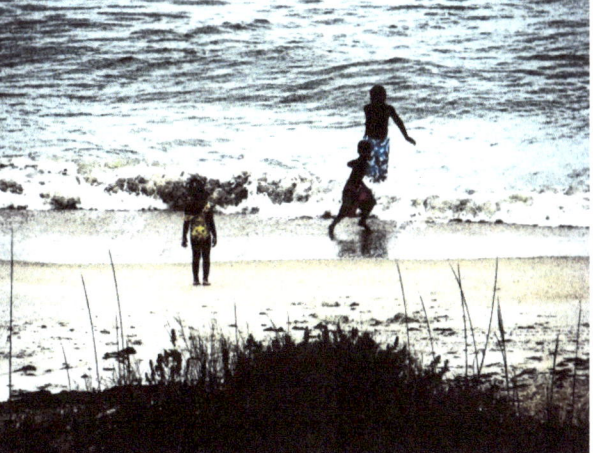

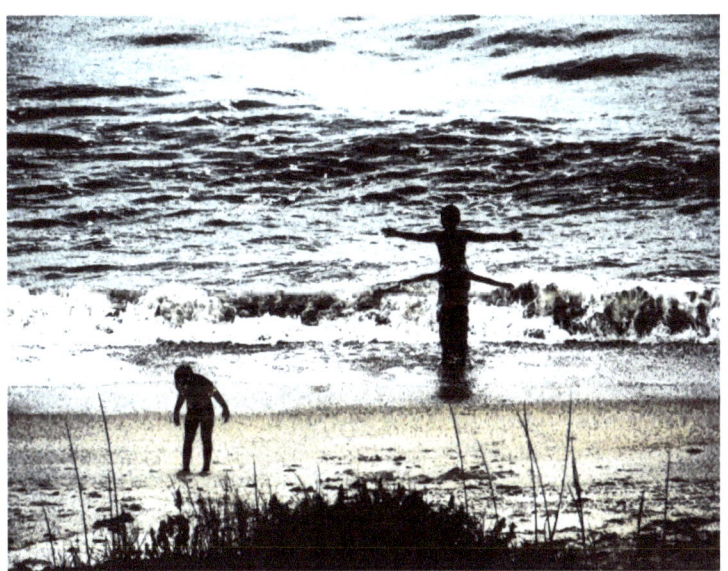

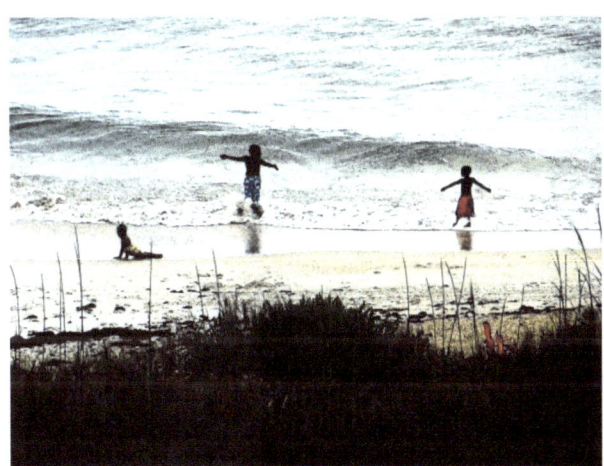 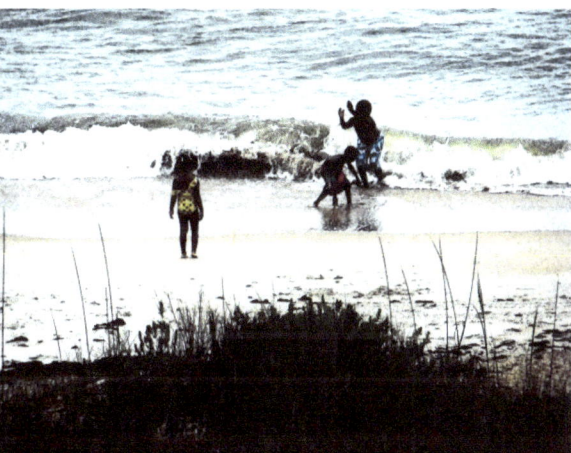

Children at Play, St. Augustine Beach, Florida, July 2014

Sailing

By: Dianne E. Woods

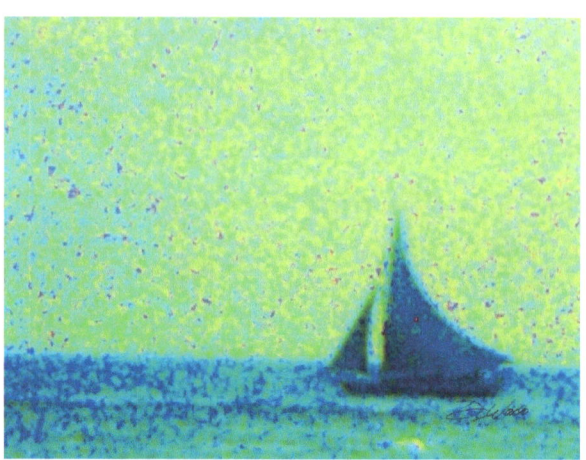

When sailing though the times of life,
I know one thing is true,
That everywhere your sails may drift,
Our Father is there too.

You never sail out of His sight,
No matter what direction,
And even when the fog is thick,
His Compass is your connection.

Les Ceyes, Haiti, August 2007

To keep us on our course of life,
Has always been His passion,
And every time you sail with Him,
Excitement is your captain.

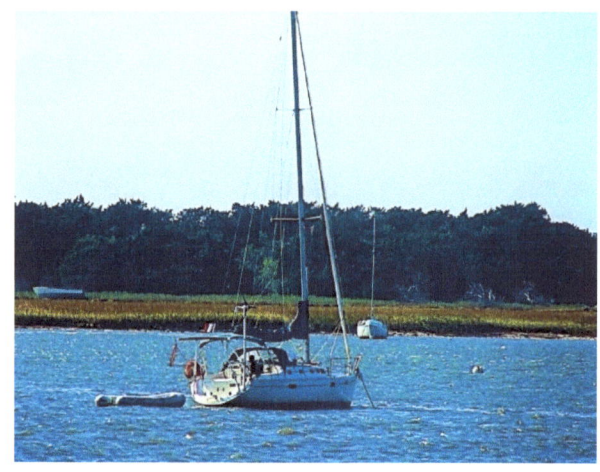

No matter where your ship may sail.
It's unique only to you.
And as He turns your rudder.
Your direction's clear and new.

When sailing through the times of life,
I know one thing is true,
That everywhere your sails may drift,
Our Father is there too.

Sailing in Fernandina Beach, Florida, November, 2011

Webster's 1828 Dictionary Definition:
Sailing: *Moving on water or in air; passing in a ship or other vessel; the act of setting sail or beginning a voyage.*
Drift: *That which is driven by wind or water.*

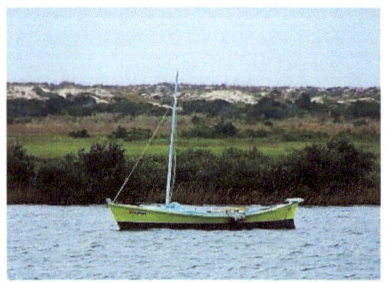 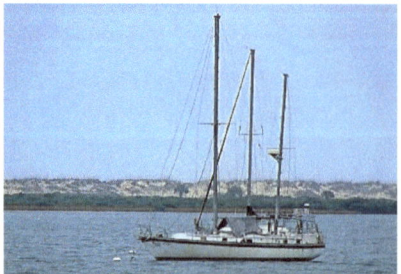 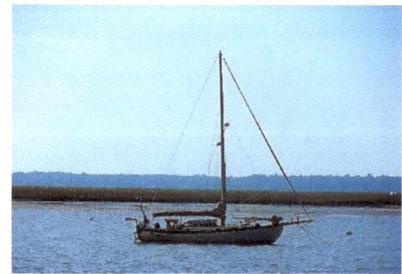

Lighthouse Beach, St. Augustine Florida, January, 2014

Poem: Sailing

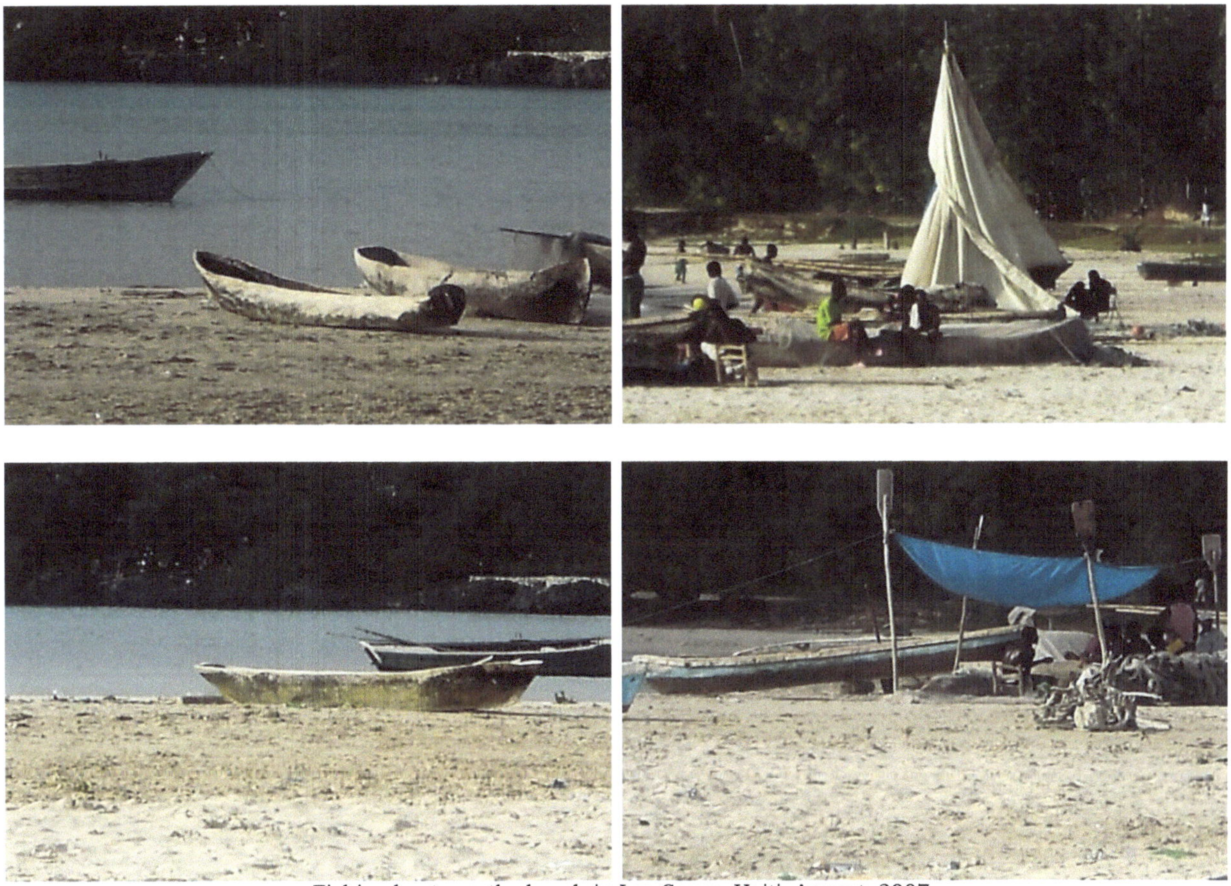

Fishing boats on the beach in Les Cayes, Haiti, August, 2007

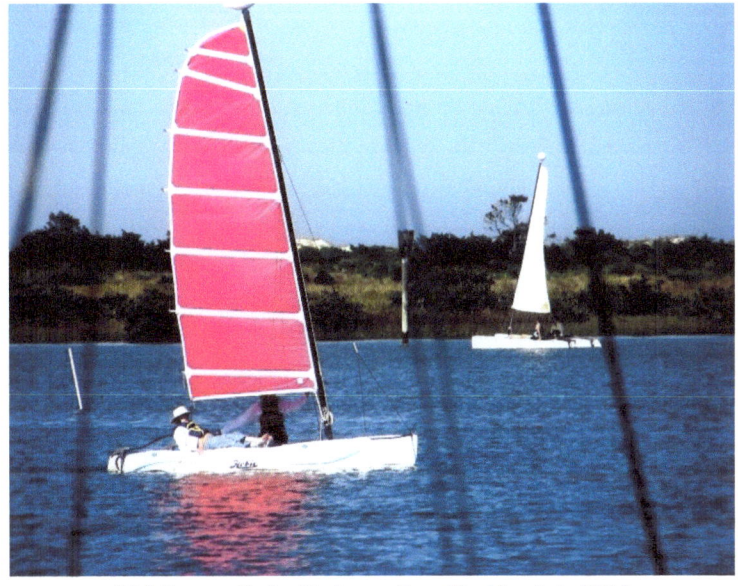

Lighthouse Park, St. Augustine, Florida, July 2014

Life and Death

By: Dianne E. Woods

I wonder why I always thought that life and death don't cross,
They have to meet, they have to greet, no matter what the cost.

It seems unfair when death takes hold, but life is always there,
To bring the fresh and new again, and help the pain we bare.

I wonder why I always thought that life and death don't cross,
They have to meet, they have to greet, no matter what the cost.

Making the most of every day, we try as best we can,
But life and death will always be, and it will never end.

I wonder why I always thought that life and death don't cross,
They have to meet, they have to greet, no matter what the cost.

Not thinking when the old is gone, there's always something new,
It changed my thoughts of life and death, and showed me a different view.

Webster's 1828 Dictionary Definition:

Life: *In a general sense, that state of animals and plants, or of an organized being, in which its natural functions and motions are performed, or in which its organs are capable of performing their functions.*

Death: *That state of a being, animal or vegetable, in which there is a total and permanent cessation of all the vital functions, when the organs have not only ceased to act, but have lost the susceptibility of renewed action.*

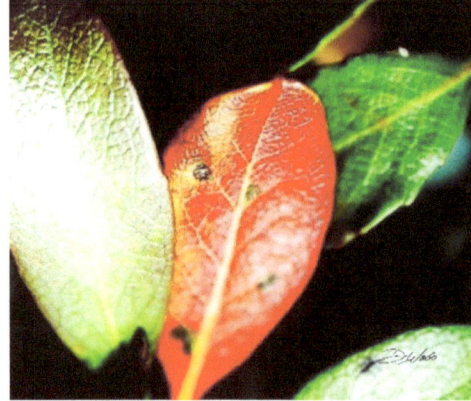

Pal Park March, 2012

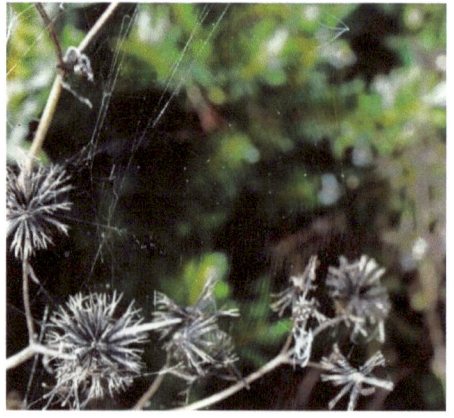

Huguenot Park, Florida, December, 2012

Poem: Life and Death

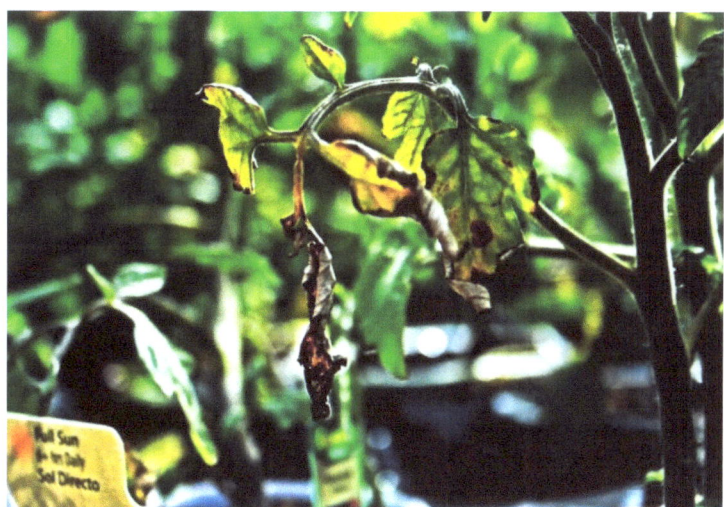

Tomato plant at a home and garden store – March, 2012

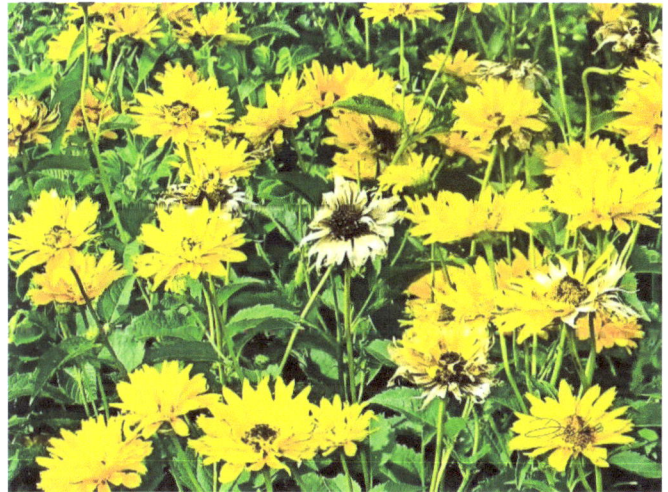

Greenville, South Carolina, June 2012

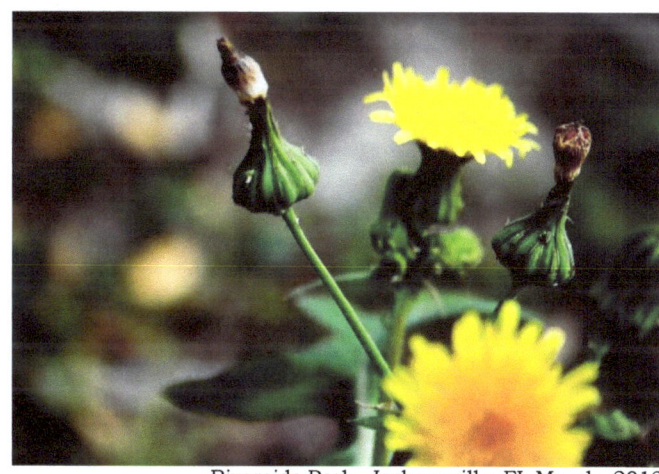

Riverside Park, Jacksonville, FL March, 2012

Imperfections

By: Dianne E. Woods

I'm beautiful just like I am,
With all my imperfections.
They are part of me, even when I don't see,
All my imperfections.

Who says I'm not my best because...
Of all my imperfections.
My gifts and talents are all mixed in,
With all my imperfections.

There are those who seek to only find,
All my imperfections.
They point, they pick, they look to change,
All my imperfections.

If only they could recognize,
That all my imperfections,
Are not imperfections at all,
But part of my PERFECTION.

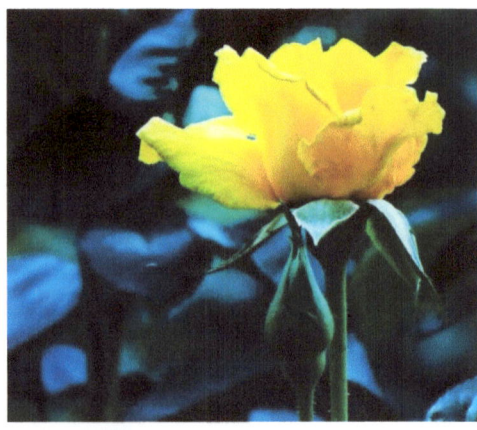

Rose Garden in South Carolina, July, 2011

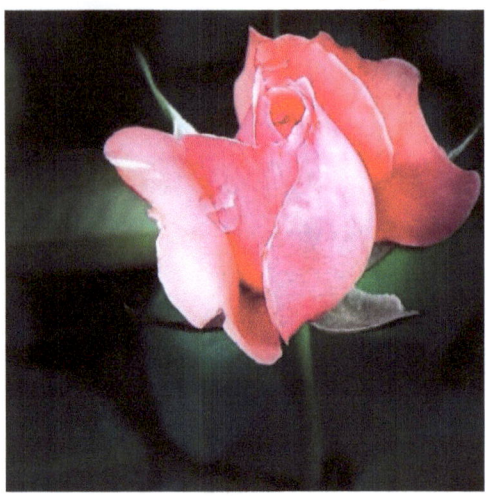

Rose Garden, South Carolina, July, 2011

Webster's 1828 Definition:
Imperfection: *Fault; the want of a part or of something necessary to complete a thing.*

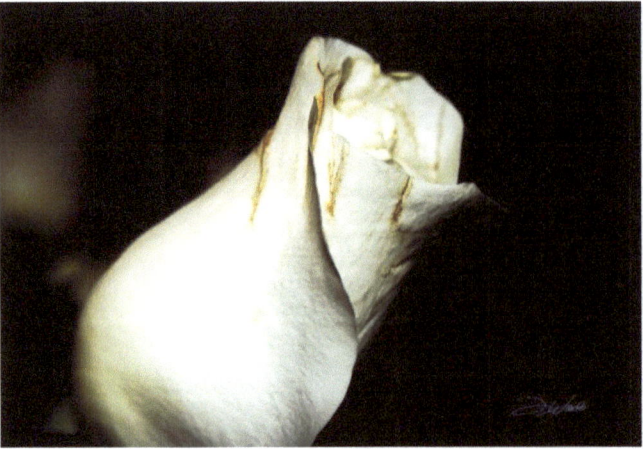

Rose Arrangement, Jacksonville, Florida, September, 2012

Poem: Imperfections

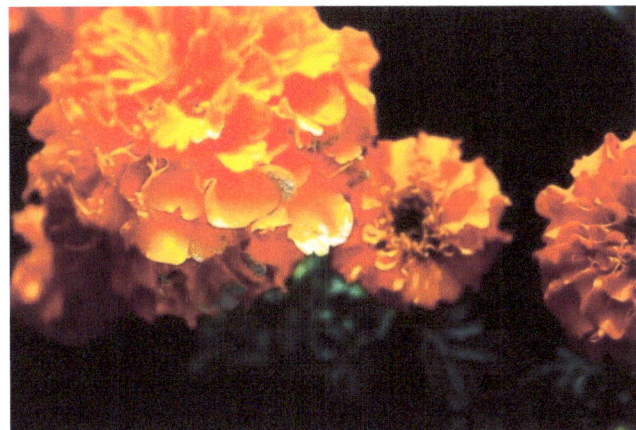

Flower Garden – March, 2012

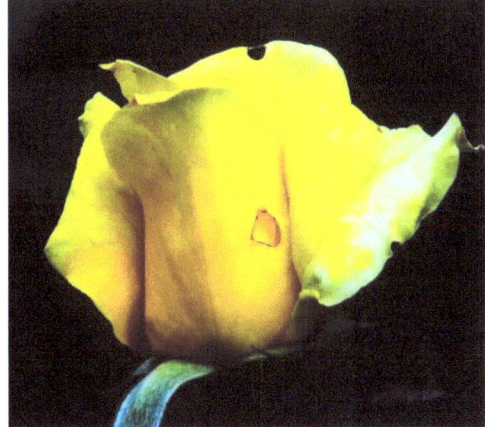

Rose Garden, South Carolina, July, 2011

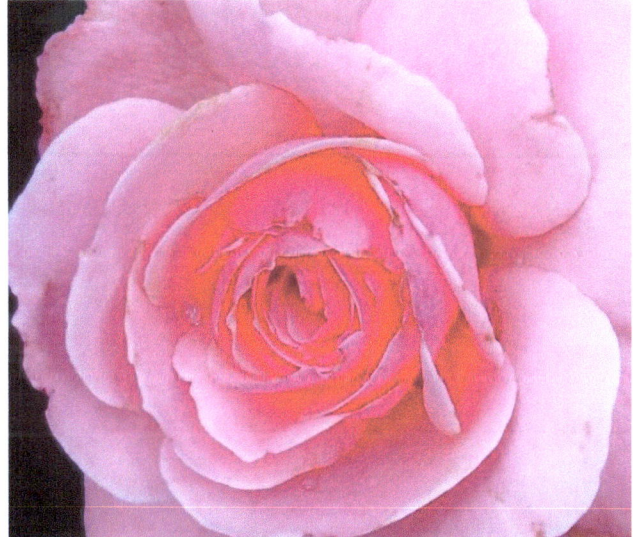

Rose Garden, South Carolina, July, 2011

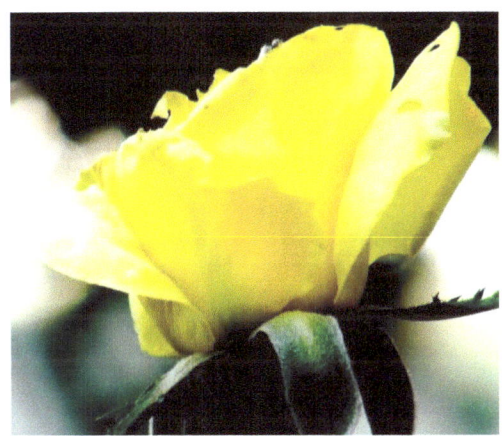

Rose Garden, South Carolina, July, 2011

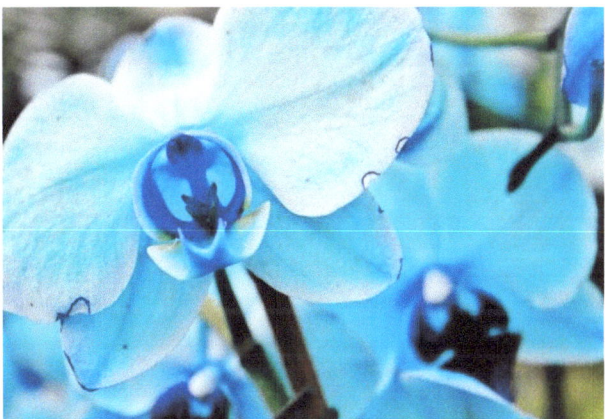

Orchid Show, Jacksonville, Florida, 2012

Feeling Unattached

By: Dianne E. Woods

I feel so unattached at times,
When things don't go just right,
Even though I've done my best,
And tried with all my might.

I feel so unattached at times,
When things don't go just right,
When working hard, and giving all,
Morning, noon and night.

What can be done, in times like these?
When things don't go just right,
Just tighten up your attitude,
Trust God and win the fight.

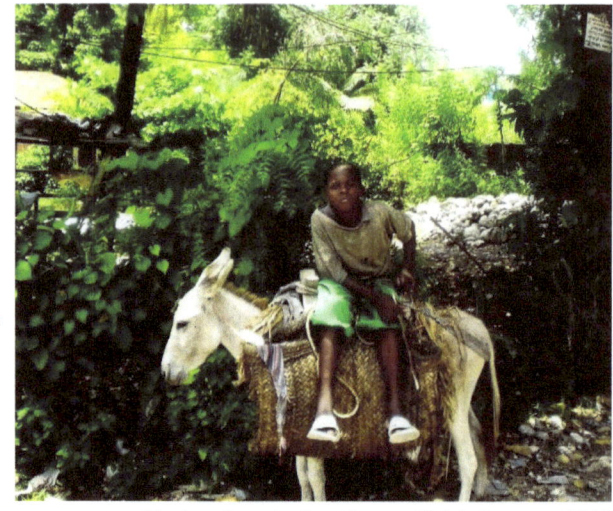

Marketplace in Les Cayes, Haiti, August, 2007

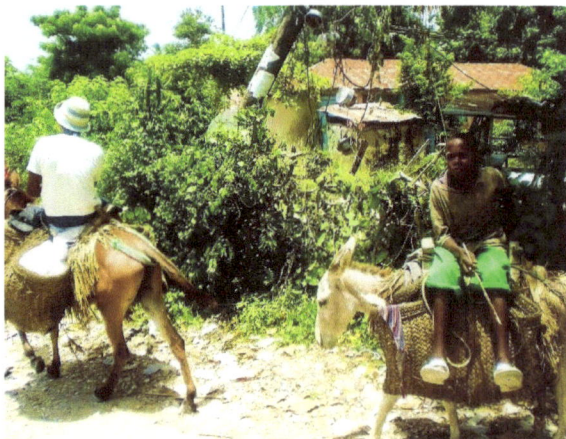

Webster's 1828 Dictionary Definition:
Unattached: *Not attached; Not closely adhering; having no fixed interest; as unattached to any party. Not united by affection.*

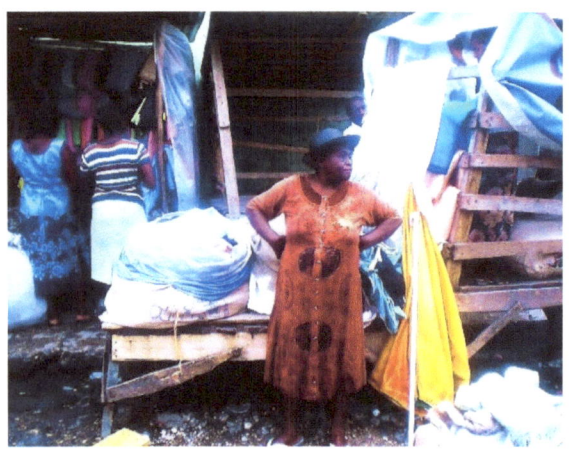

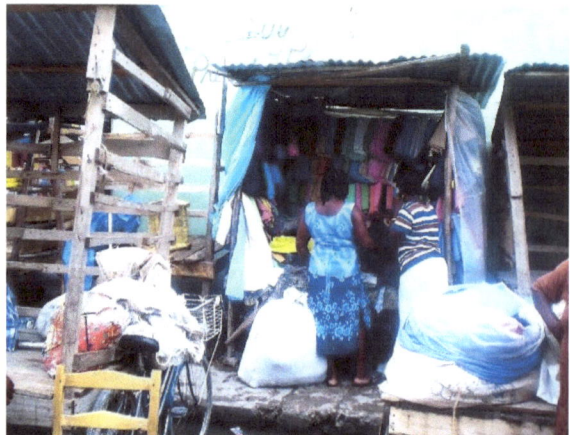

Marketplace in Les Cayes, Haiti, August, 2007

Poem: Feeling Unattached

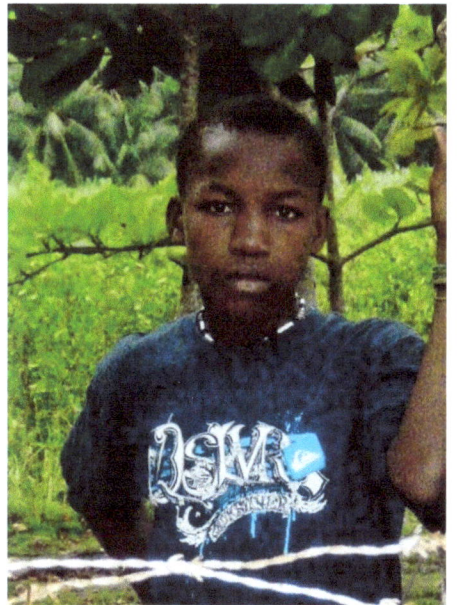 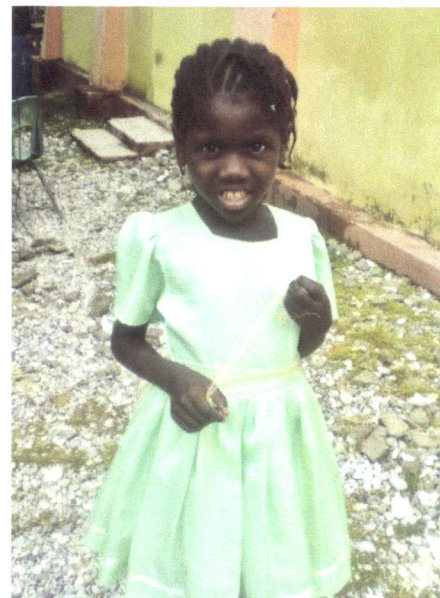

Children in Les Cayes, Haiti, August 2007

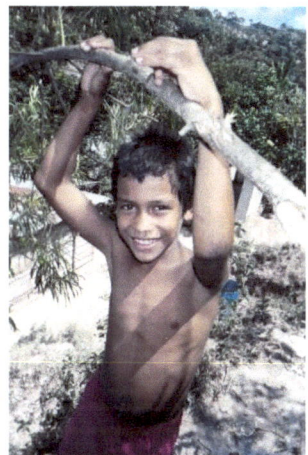

Mountains of Honduras, August 2006

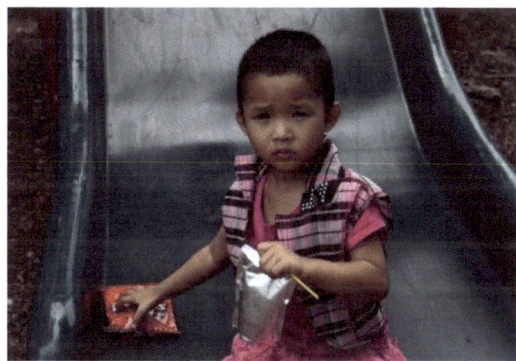

Burmese Child, Jacksonville, Florida, June, 2012

It's All in the Details
By Dianne E. Woods

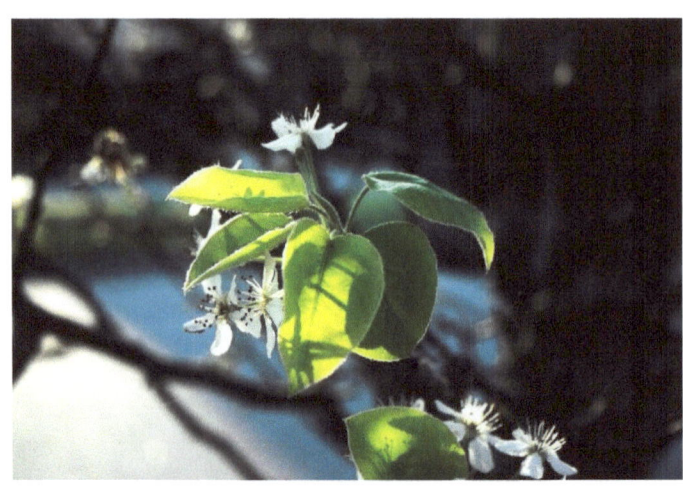

It's all in the details,
Can't you see,
My beauty, my image,
Created to be.

It's all in the details,
Can't you see,
My joy and my splendor,
But not just for me.

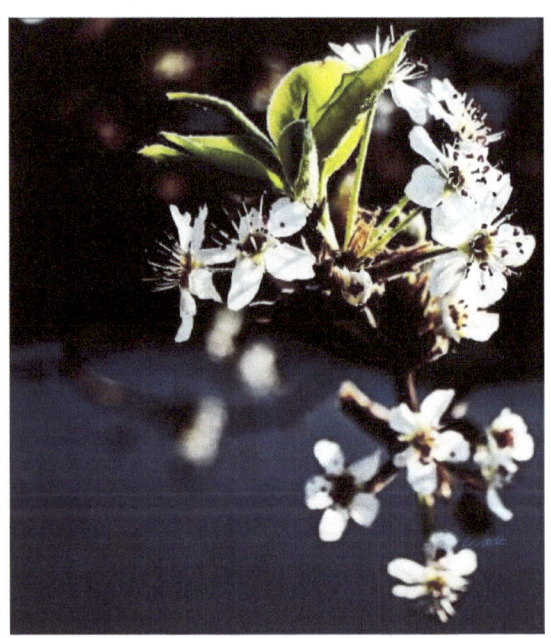

It's all in the details,
Can't you see,
Each petal, each leaf,
So fleeting, so free.

It's all in the details,
Can't you see,
Created by God,
For you and for me.

Webster's 1828 Dictionary Definition

Detail: *To relate, report or narrate in particulars; to recite the particulars of; to particularize; to relate minutely and distinctly; as, he detailed all the facts in due order.*

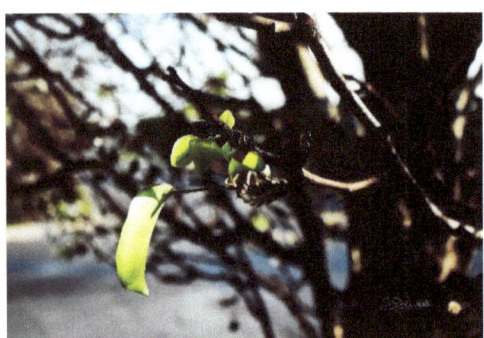

Cherry Blossom Tree, Valdosta, Georgia, March, 2012

Poem: It's All in the Details

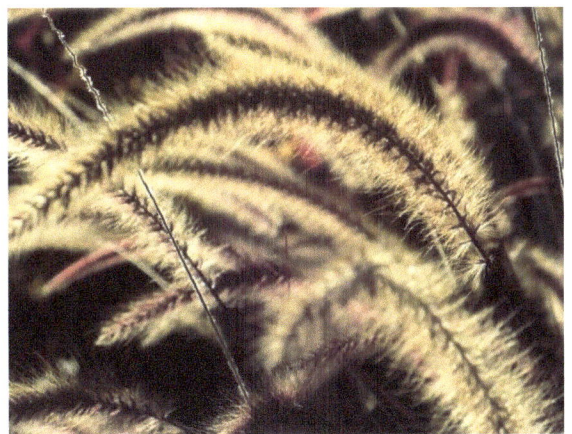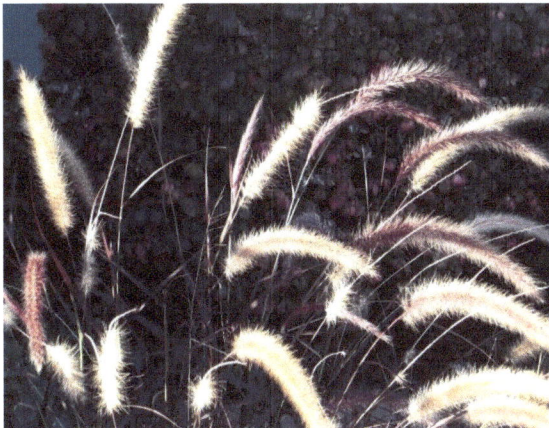

Jacksonville, Florida, October, 2007

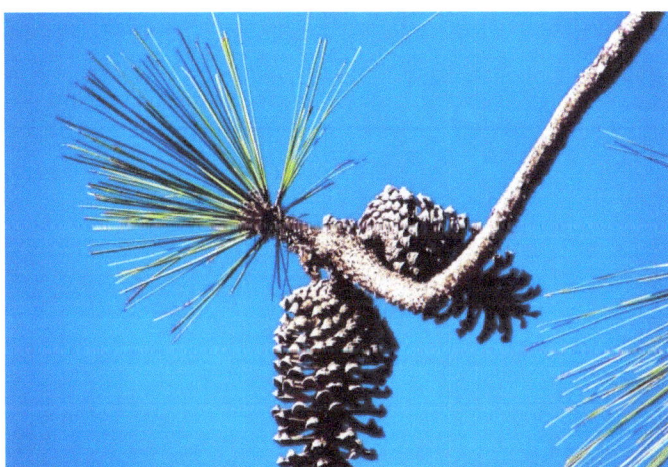

Pal Park, Jacksonville, Florida, December, 2013

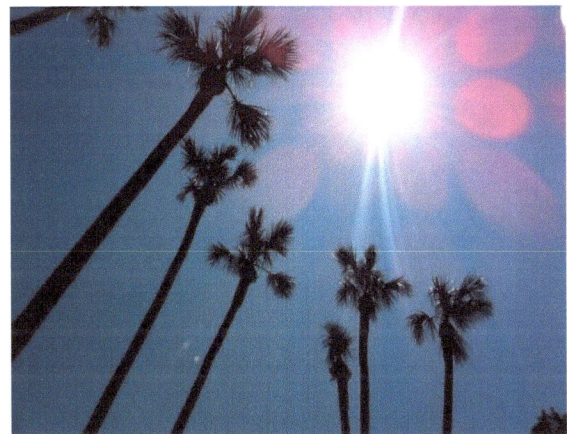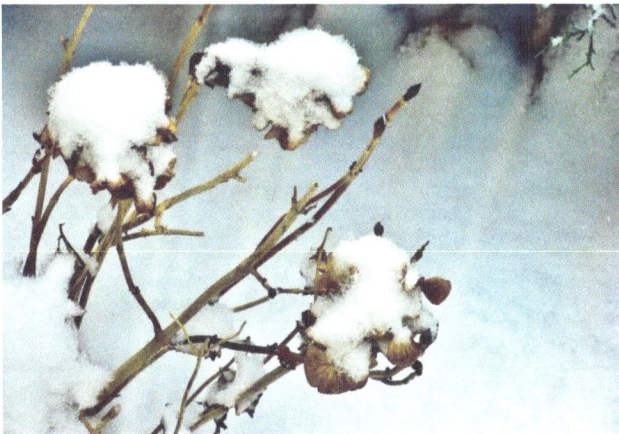

Golf Course, Florida, August, 2012   Mom and Dads, Inkster, Michigan, 2014

Okay, I Think I've Got It!

By: Dianne E. Woods

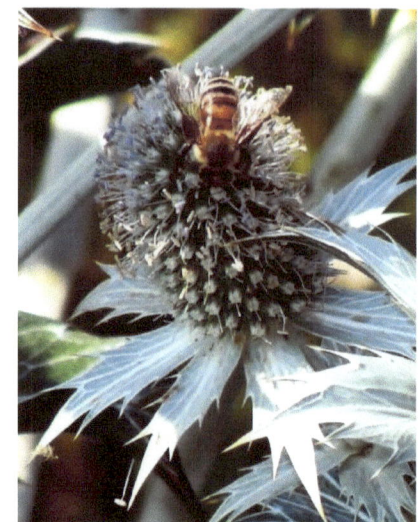

South Carolina, July, 2011

"Okay, I think I've got it"!
We often sometimes say,
When understanding questions,
As we grow up every day.

"Okay, I think I've got it"!
What more can be achieved,
Our wonderment keeps growing,
To fulfil our every need.

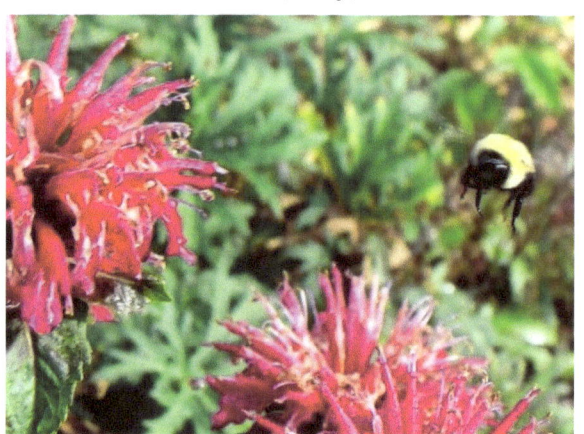

Jacksonville, Florida, July, 2013

"Okay, I think I've got it"!
Our choices must be clear,
To go this way or that way,
Even when we fear.

"Okay, I think I've got it"!
Will never ever end,
As long as we keep living
And let learning be our friend.

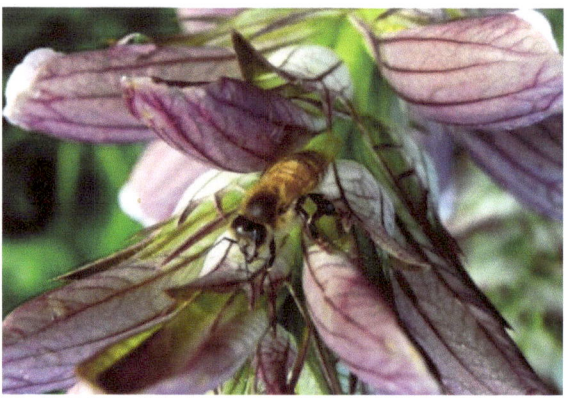

Jacksonville, Florida, July, 2013

Webster's 1828 Dictionary

It: *A substitute or pronoun of the neuter gender, sometimes called demonstrative, and standing for anything except males and females,*

Poem: Okay I Think I've Got It!

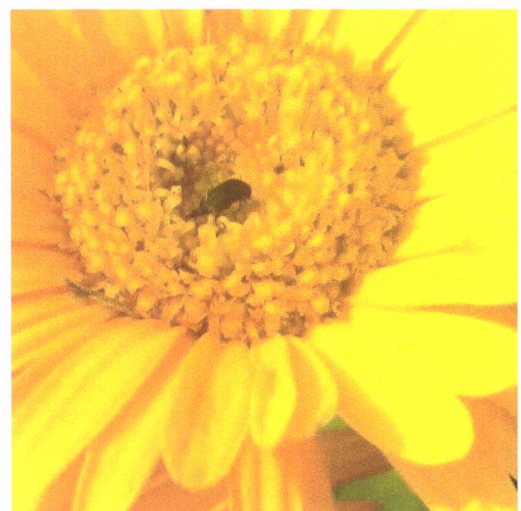
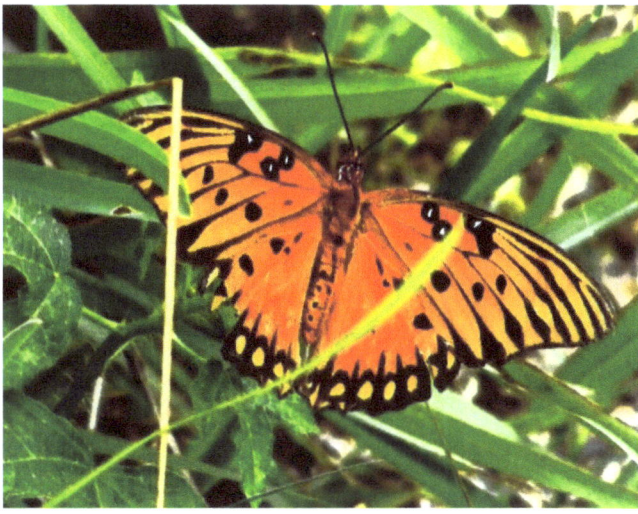

Photographed, July 7, 2011

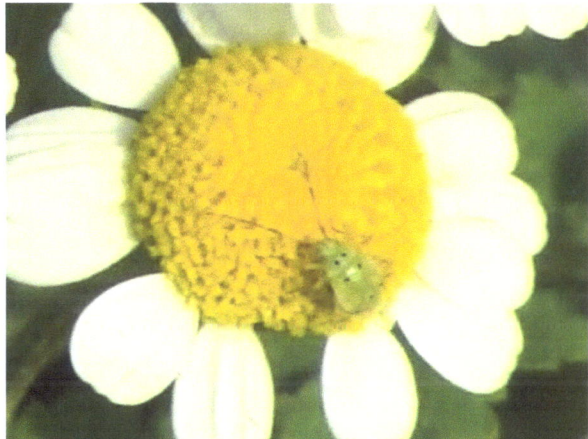

Photographed, July 7, 2011

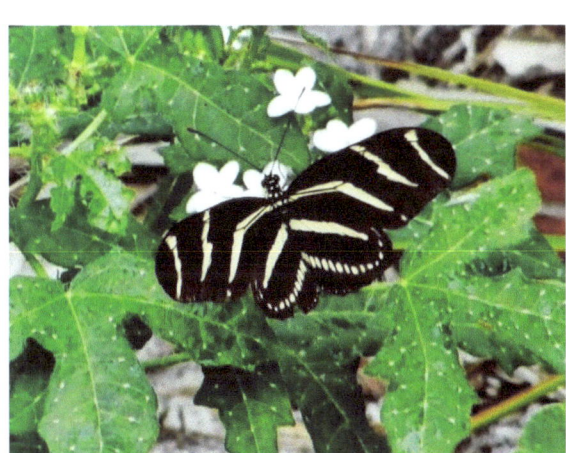
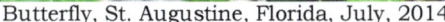

Butterfly, St. Augustine, Florida, July, 2014

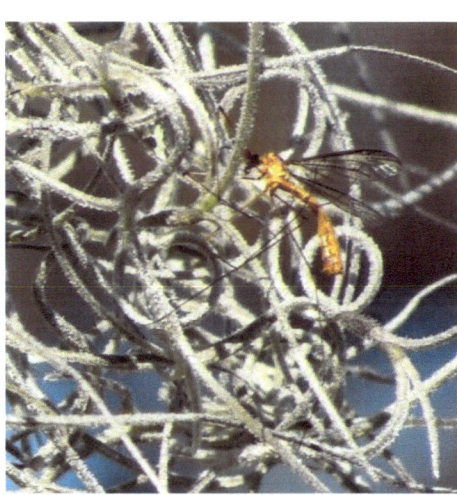

Jacksonville, Florida, December, 2013

About the Author and Photographer

Greetings readers! My name is Dianne Elizabeth Thompson-Woods and I am please you have taken the time to view my work. I was born in Detroit, Michigan, and raised in Inkster, a suburb of Detroit and currently reside in Jacksonville, Fl. My love for the arts and music has always been nurtured from an early age by my parents, Eugene and Bernice Thompson, who at the publishing of this work in 2014 celebrated a healthy 91 years of life, and 65 years of marriage. In addition to my love of photography, I play classical flute and love singing.

My desire is to touch the lives of others through my photography and poetry. My fine arts style of photography primarily focuses on nature and landscape capturing moments in time that are unique and writing poetry to help spark the imagination. Many of my photographs were taken during my travels to Honduras, Haiti, The Dominican Republic, Bulgaria, France, Peru, and Israel where I make it a point to find and embrace the natural beauty that surrounds me during my travels.

My deep desire is to continue traveling, writing, and "capturing creation as it happens" from around the world. I hope you spend time interpreting the poems and pondering on each image and allow them to speak to your heart and notice the details and beauty of that moment in time. Have a great one!

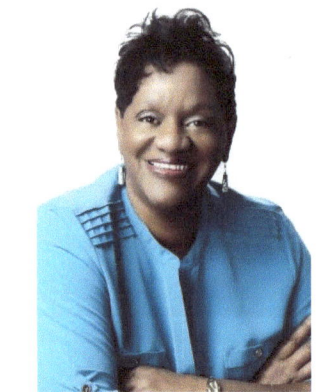

Dianne E. Woods